Beyond Cinderella

THE MODERN WOMAN'S GUIDE
TO FINDING A PRINCE

Additional copies available through:
Beyond Cinderella
P.O. Box 51204
Seattle, WA 98115-1204

or call 1-800-445-MATE
in Washington State call 206-328-7840

BEYOND CINDERELLA, THE MODERN WOMAN'S GUIDE TO FINDING A PRINCE.
Copyright 1987 by Nita Tucker with Debra Feinstein. All rights reserved. Printed in the United
States of America. No part of this book may be used or reproduced in any manner whatsoever
without written permission from the author.
First edition, first printing. April 1987.
Printed and published by
Outdoor Empire Publishing, Inc.,
Seattle, Washington.

Library of Congress Cataloging-in-Publication Data
Tucker, Nita
Beyond Cinderella,
The Modern Woman's Guide To Finding A Prince.
Library of congress Catalog Card Number: 87-61337
ISBN 0-916682-57-9

This book is dedicated to my Prince, Tony.

Acknowledgements

Thank you,

To JODI ANABLE for loving and taking care of my most favorite little person, Jordan. To TERRY and ALAN AXELROD for always letting me know I could do it and for being role models for a successful, lasting relationship. To KAY BUCK for being there in the beginning. To DAVID and NANCY EDELSTEIN and LANNY FRENCH for giving their magic touch to this book. To DEBRA FEINSTEIN for believing in the book and for her dedication and brilliance in making it happen. To PAUL FISHER for making me always feel I have family. To CAROL LADD for being there when I needed her. To NANCY DIANE MANELLI for sticking with me and doing whatever it took. To JEANNE McKNIGHT for being a success in finding a lifetime mate and for her love and encouragement. To PAIGE GRANT PELL for her outstanding work in the area of relationships. To KAREN RAMSEY for believing in me and supporting me so this book would happen. To CAROLE SCHURCH for being a great friend and doing anything and everything to support this book. And to TONY TUCKER for making my life better than I ever dreamed it could be.

I also wish to thank all the people who have taken "Connecting" for applying what I've taught and making it work in their lives, and the staffs of the AXELROD COMPANY and EDELSTEIN ASSOCIATES for all their support.

— Nita Tucker

Thank you,

To VIVIAN and BERNIE FEINSTEIN for their support, love and for the way they pitched in. To FRAC FOX for her commitment and outstanding help, and for being such a fun person to work with. To DOROTHY HARDY for her love, wisdom, support, and generosity, without which I could not have written this book. To BOB JOHNSON for being a wonderful friend and for his valuable help on the book. To CHRIS KEEBLER for her encouragement and support. To ANTOINETTE PORTIS for applying her exceptional insight and talent to this book, and for being the best "best friend" I can imagine. To NITA TUCKER, for giving me the opportunity to write this book with her, for inspiring me, and for using her wisdom, compassion, and humor to make a contribution to people's lives and their relationships.

— Debra Feinstein

Both authors wish to thank our outstanding editors who made this book much better than it could have been without them: JODI ANABLE, ALAN AXELROD, TERRY AXELROD, DEBORAH FOX, FRAC FOX, BOB JOHNSON, DOROTHY HARDY, ANTOINETTE PORTIS, SUSAN REANIER, and SUSIE ROBBINS. We also wish to thank WERNER ERHARD for what he has taught us and FRIDA WEISMAN and JULIE MURPHY of OUTDOOR EMPIRE PUBLISHING, INC. for making the impossible happen and making it seem easy.

Table of Contents

INTRODUCTION 1

Before You Set Out On Your Quest
THERE ARE SOME THINGS YOU NEED TO KNOW

1. SOMEDAY YOUR PRINCE WILL COME? 9
   Waiting for the prince to find you has gotten you
   nowhere, so you better start looking for him.

2. DROP THE VEIL OF SECRECY 19
   Wanting a relationship is nothing to be ashamed of,
   so come out of the closet.

3. BEYOND SLEEPING BEAUTY 27
   By postponing your life until your prince shows up,
   you could be delaying his arrival.

4. FROGS THAT DON'T TURN INTO PRINCES 41
   Hanging around with Mr. Wrong will not lead you to
   Mr. Right.

5. FROGS THAT DO TURN INTO PRINCES 55
   Being too sure you know "your type" could keep you
   from recognizing the real thing when it comes along.

6. GLASS SLIPPERS COME IN ALL SIZES 63
   If you're not finding great men, maybe it's because
   you don't know how to look for them.

Slaying The Dragons
HOW TO RECOGNIZE AND OVERCOME THE OBSTACLES

7. BREAK THE CURSE 79
   Close encounters of the wrong kind may be keeping
   you from finding the right kind.

8. PUMPKINS AND OTHER PROBLEMS 91
If you don't like the way your relationships have been
turning out . . . try turning within.

9. WHEN YOU'RE KNOCKED OFF YOUR STEED 111
You can't avoid rejection, but you *can* learn how to
handle it.

10. THINGS YOUR FAIRY GODMOTHER NEVER
TOLD YOU 123
When "going all the way" gets in the way.

11. HOW TO CAPTURE A PRINCE 131
Cages and traps won't hold a man's heart.

Living Happily Ever After
THE TECHNOLOGY OF MAKING
YOUR DREAMS COME TRUE

12. TRY A LITTLE ALCHEMY 145
Intimacy is the key that unlocks the treasure within.

13. WAVE YOUR MAGIC WAND 153
You've got a tool for making your relationships
miraculous.

14. CLAIM YOUR CROWN 167
Transform yourself into the woman you've always
wanted to be.

15. LEAD A CHARMED LIFE 183
If you could have the kind of relationship you really
wanted, what would it be like?

16. BRING ON THE SUITORS 193
With a world of resources at your fingertips, finding a
prince has never been so easy.

17. "THE END?" 203
No, just the last chapter before the beginning.

Introduction

ONCE UPON A TIME . . . women did not need a book to help them find men. But social conditions affecting relationships between the sexes have undergone more changes over the last three decades than they usually do in three centuries.

The culture in which men and women live today is very different from the one in which our parents grew up: The pill. The sexual revolution. Baby boomers and the mess they made of the woman-to-man ratio. Women's liberation. The skyrocketing divorce rate. The trend toward mating later in life. The marriage squeeze. The Phil Donahue show. These are just some of the factors that have led to a new order (some say chaos) between men and women.

You, as a single woman over 25 (I'm guessing), are both a cause and an effect of this new order. Your lifetime spans the "before" and "after" of this radical cultural change.

During the early part of your life you learned all about mating the way it used to be. That's when you first got the idea that someday, your prince would find you.

Then one day when you weren't paying attention, the game changed. Things were suddenly different. They started to get confusing and they never stopped.

First, you lost interest in settling down and got involved in your career and other things instead. When you went back to look for a man, there didn't seem to be any good ones left. Then there was that awful study that said that because you had waited too long, you were going to end up an old maid.

On top of that, relationships don't seem to be as easy as they once were. You wonder whether you will ever be capable of having a good one, and sometimes, you question whether you even want one.

How to find a relationship at the age of 25+ in today's world is something that your mother couldn't have told you

1

about even if she had wanted to. This is a game that almost no one knows how to play, let alone win. That's why you need a book.

WHO THIS BOOK IS FOR

This book is for single women who think they might or know they do want a lasting relationship with a man.

By a relationship I do not necessarily mean marriage. I do mean a partnership that is loving, supportive, nurturing, committed, romantic, satisfying, and with a PRINCE.

By a prince I do not mean the fantasy hero with whom you're destined to spend your life. I mean a real human being, one with strengths and weaknesses. It is my contention that there are many men, not just one or two, with whom you can experience passion, romance, happiness, and lasting love.

It has become unfashionable for women to say that they want a relationship. When asked if they do, they are apt to respond with, "I've got a terrific job and many close friends. I'm happy, so no, I don't need a relationship." This is like being asked if you want a convertible and answering "no, I have a new set of dishes and my stereo works great — I don't need a car."

That you want a relationship doesn't necessarily mean you feel desperate about not having one or that your life is miserable without one. You could be having a great life and still want someone to share it with. That's perfectly natural.

WHAT THIS BOOK COVERS

Since what you find will be influenced by what you are looking for, the first section of this book deals with your attitudes and expectations about finding a relationship. It will help you start your quest on the right foot.

Because relationships are so often a series of false starts

and unhappy endings, the second section covers what to do with a man once you find him. It teaches you how to overcome the obstacles you will be likely to encounter on the way to living happily ever after.

The third section offers tools and techniques for making relationships the fulfilling, satisfying, exciting, inspiring, passionate adventures they were meant to be.

This book is action oriented. It is based on the premise that in today's world if you want something, you have to go after it. Once you finish this book, your days of waiting for a prince will be history.

HOW TO READ THIS BOOK

This book identifies many of the counterproductive attitudes and behaviors that women have adopted with respect to relationships, and it prescribes more effective ways of thinking and acting. Given the way all the rules got switched on you, it would be a miracle if there isn't *something* in your approach to relationships that needs to be fixed.

The best attitude to have in reading this book is one of willingness to discover what you are doing ineffectively and what you can do to correct it.

HOW TO PUT THE MOST INTO THIS BOOK

This is a workbook. There are exercises and assignments throughout it. If you complete the exercises and carry out the assignments, you *will* find a relationship. If you skip the exercises and assignments you may get results anyway, but who knows? You will get the most out of this book by putting the most into it.

The assignments are organized into a six-week plan. This plan is the "action" part of the book, the part where you put its principles into practice.

It is assumed you will finish reading the book within a short time frame, then go on to begin this six-week plan, which is outlined at the end of the last chapter. If you like, you may instead begin carrying out the assignments as you encounter them in your reading.

These assignments are every bit as important as the data in the book. They are what will enable you to reach your goal. I can't emphasize enough how essential it is for you to complete them if you want to find a relationship.

WHO I AM AND
WHAT LED ME TO WRITE THIS BOOK

Lots of people meet, fall in love, and get married. They're the naturals, the ones to whom "it just happens." I was not a natural in the area of relationships, and that is a key to my success as a teacher.

If you ask a natural skier to describe how to ski, he or she will tell you to just wiggle your hips and go down the mountain. This is not a big help to most of us.

I have a friend who is a natural in the area of relationships. She met a man as he walked off an elevator. It was love at first sight and they soon got married. But if you ask her how to find a relationship, all she can tell you to do is to wait outside an elevator.

The best kind of teacher is someone who understands the principles of her subject. Because I was not a natural in the area of relationships, I had to take a series of purposeful steps to find someone and to establish a successful relationship with him.

I didn't realize it at the time, but in retrospect I can see that not only was I was taking steps to find a relationship for myself, I was also developing a "curriculum" for others to follow. When friends saw that I had the kind of relationship I had always wanted, they began asking me for advice. My background as a teacher, seminar leader, and consultant provided me with the skills to extrapolate from my experiences a set of principles that they could easily follow.

I talked to a lot of people — men and women — about what I had done and what I had discovered. Many of them took the steps and applied the techniques I told them about. What had worked for me also worked for them — they, too, found relationships. They demonstrated that the principles I had discovered were universal.

Word spread, and I began receiving phone calls from all over the country from people seeking advice about how to find relationships. It was obvious that this was information a lot of people wanted.

Something else was obvious, too. For many people, not having a partner was a source of tremendous pain. I had been through this pain myself, so whenever people called I found the time to talk with them. I understood what they were going through and I knew that the information I had could help them.

I decided to create a course as a way of making this information more widely available and so that I could put down the phone once in awhile. In October of 1985, I taught the first "Connecting: How to Find A Lifetime Relationship" seminar in Seattle, Washington.

Since then, hundreds of women and men have taken this course and have gone on to find satisfying relationships. My work with them has proven to me that anyone who is willing to take the necessary steps can find a lifetime partner.

If you want a relationship, you *can* have one. You *can* realize your dreams. Just keep reading.

Before You Set Out On Your Quest
There are some things you need to know.

1

Someday Your Prince Will Come?

WAITING FOR THE PRINCE TO FIND YOU HAS GOTTEN YOU NOWHERE, SO YOU BETTER START LOOKING FOR HIM.

Successful salespeople don't talk about their prospects showing up "when the timing is right."

You don't hear bankers or stockbrokers saying they find the best investment opportunities when they're "not looking for them."

And no executive I've ever met advocates letting the success of her company "just happen."

Yet many of these same women believe a relationship just happens — when they're ready — when the timing is right — when they're not looking for one. It's the reason so many women who are successful in their professions are unsuccessful in the area of relationships.

Do you believe that a relationship will "just happen" when the timing is right? Do you believe you'll find a man when you're "not looking" for one?

Maybe you can point to someone you know who met her future spouse while she was taking out the garbage. The question is, how is that going to help you?

There's probably a salesperson somewhere who met a customer while waiting to use a pay phone, but it isn't likely she decided to wait outside phone booths as a strategy for making future sales. You've tried waiting for the prince to show up and he hasn't; now you need a strategy, an action plan for finding him.

Salespeople know that not every prospect turns into a customer, so they call on prospect after prospect. They consider themselves successful if one out of every dozen signs an order. Likewise, because not every man you date is going to be a prince, you're going to have to go out with lots of men.

Here's how it works: You date a variety of men. Those who aren't the prince disqualify themselves or you disqualify them. The man who doesn't disqualify himself or get disqualified by you is the prince.

In order to date a lot of men you've got to meet even more men. You don't meet men at home, so you have to go out and find them.

It's simple, it's logical, it makes sense; and it's a lot more efficient than waiting for Mr. Right to walk by while you're taking the garbage out. But you don't like it, right? You're turned off by the idea of having to do something to find a man.

Why is it that women who make things happen rather than wait for them to happen in all other areas of their lives insist on "doing nothing" to find a relationship?

WHERE THE BOYS WERE

One reason is that at one time, "doing nothing" worked. Back when you were in school, you met guys wherever you went — in the chemistry lab, in class, at football games. If you went to an all-girls school you met them at the hamburger stand, at the shopping center, at mixers. Back then, you didn't have to make any special effort to form relationships.

But if you think about it, you weren't really "doing nothing." You were constantly participating in activities — dances, parties, mixers, sports events, club meetings — that brought you into contact with members of the opposite sex.

The "spontaneous" relationships you had in school were actually the result of an enormous amount of socializing. You just didn't notice you were socializing because it was what everyone was doing, all the time.

School was the ideal environment for connecting with the opposite sex: everyone was in the same age group, everyone was single, and everyone was looking. To meet people, all you had to do was show up every day.

Now that people are waiting until they're older to mate, those social situations they once took for granted are no longer so prevalent or convenient. In the absence of the ideal mating conditions of school, just showing up at work each day is not going to provide opportunities for meeting new people. If you want to meet men, you have to make a special effort to put yourself in situations where you'll come in contact with them.

POOR EXCUSES

There are a lot of other reasons why "doing nothing" is so popular:

1. It keeps you from feeling responsible.
2. You're lazy.
3. You're too busy.
4. You're scared.
5. You don't like "the dating scene."

6. You want to avoid rejection, discomfort, embarrassment.
7. You don't want to waste your time.
8. Inertia — you're comfortable with things the way they are.
9. You don't know how to go about looking.
10. It isn't romantic.
11. Your reason: _____

Convincing though these excuses may be, they're not keeping you warm at night. I've worked with hundreds of women and not one has ever had a man come to her door and say, "I'm the prince and I'm looking for a woman who would like to have a relationship with me. Does such a woman live here?"

WHAT ABOUT ROMANCE?

Many women feel going out and looking for men is a bad idea because it isn't spontaneous or romantic. But who says it has to be? For starters — your parents, your friends, and almost everyone else you know, most of whom subscribe to the "you shouldn't have to look" theory of mating. This notion is reinforced by movies and television, the source of many of our most cherished myths about relationships.

We've been taught all our lives that relationships should unfold in a spontaneous, romantic way. "Going out and looking" just doesn't seem romantic. Okay, maybe it's not, but staying home alone isn't either.

You can't have a romantic relationship until you meet someone, so let's get our priorities straight. Let's handle meeting someone, then let's worry about making it romantic.

BEYOND WISHING AND HOPING

I was once a big believer in waiting for a relationship. I

waited for about five years before I figured out that my approach wasn't working. Then I changed my strategy from waiting, wishing, and hoping to taking purposeful action, and four months later I found a relationship.

Here's how it happened:

I was in Bali, one of the most romantic countries in the world. I had met a man who was tall, good-looking, sensitive, fun — and a doctor! I recognized him immediately — he was the man I had been waiting for.

We were walking along a ridge overlooking a beautiful vista. The sunset was magnificent. He looked into my eyes; I looked up into his, ready for our first kiss. He said three magic words, words that were to change the direction of my life. They were "Nita, I'm gay." (I'm not kidding — this really happened!)

I saw my future flash before me. An ancient Chinese proverb says,"If we do not change our direction, we are likely to end up where we are headed." I saw that my fantasizing and hoping had gotten me nowhere and that unless I did something else, I was likely to end up alone.

Right then and there I made a commitment. I resolved to find a relationship. I didn't know what it would take but I was going to find out, and I was going to do it.

I had a great life in San Francisco. I had a successful career, terrific friends, a comfortable home. But I knew I wasn't going to meet the prince there. I did some research and learned that Seattle was a good place to meet single men. I decided to move there.

I went back to San Francisco, sold my house, got all my belongings together, and moved to Seattle. I began applying the same kind of energy and perseverence that had made me successful in business to my new project, that of finding a relationship.

I did everything I could think of. I told everyone I met that I was looking for a relationship and asked them if they knew anyone with whom they could fix me up. I went to every party I could find and to art galleries, restaurants, bars, and other places where I thought the kind of men I wanted to meet would go. I went out three or four nights a week.

Was it fun? Of course not. The only people who think the

dating scene is fun are people who are married.

Was it worth it? Absolutely. I met a man with whom I fell madly in love. We've been happily married for the last five years.

PROJECT: RELATIONSHIP

I'm not saying you have to move to a new city and do everything I did in order to find a relationship. What I am saying is that you have to make a commitment to reaching your goal and to taking whatever action is necessary to reach it. In other words, you have to make this a project.

There's a difference between "making something a project" and "hoping it will turn out." The difference is in your level of commitment and in your responsibility for reaching your goal.

For example, when it comes to going out to meet men, women can be very picky. "I'd like to have a relationship, but I wouldn't be caught dead at a singles event," you say. "I want to meet Mr. Right but I don't like blind dates."

If your goal is to become vice-president of your company, you don't say, "No way I'm going anywhere near a client meeting," or "I'd never go to a bank function," or "I refuse to meet with the sales team." If you plan on becoming a concert pianist you don't say, "But I don't have time to practice" or "I refuse to play scales."

Another characteristic of a project is that when you undertake it, you assume there will be a tangible end result and that you will reach this goal.

For example, when you set out to buy a house, you expect to end up with a house. When you enroll in school to become a real estate agent, you expect to get your license. When you decide to open up a branch office, you know one will open.

The question with a project isn't *whether* something will happen at the end, but *how* and *when* it will happen.

We accept that the project approach is effective in other

fields of endeavor, but we think finding a relationship is somehow different. It's not. We need to adopt the same attitude toward finding a relationship that we would toward any other important undertaking.

RULES FOR A PROJECT

Think of a time you took on a project. You may not have realized it, but if the project was successful, you were probably following these basic principles:

1. You made time for it, made it a priority.
2. Every step you took had the purpose of getting you closer to your goal.
3. You didn't make excuses.
4. You were sure you would reach your goal, and you kept it in sight.
5. You came up with a plan that had milestones you needed to reach along the way.
6. You took risks when necessary.
7. You worked at the project even when you didn't feel like it.
8. Getting rejected didn't stop you from taking the next step.
9. You were willing to try anything that could forward your project.
10. You didn't give up even when you felt discouraged.

My success came when I stopped thinking of a relationship as something that was in the hands of fate and started thinking of it as a project that was under my control. Yours, too, will come when you take on "Project: Relationship" and transfer the skills that have made you successful in other areas of your life to realizing your goal of finding a mate.

If you're not convinced, ask yourself how long you have been waiting for the prince to show up on your doorstep. How much longer are you willing to wait?

STOP WHINING ABOUT TIME

I know you're busy and you don't have time for a new project.

I can't tell you how many women in my courses started out saying they didn't have time to go out and meet men. A lot of them were even busier than you are. Once they became convinced that putting in time would be necessary, however, each and every one of them found they were able to fit "looking for a relationship" into their schedules. You can too.

Besides, if you were in a relationship, you would have to find time to spend with your mate. Get into the habit of making time for a relationship now.

A LITTLE HELP FROM A FRIEND

The first thing to do once you make a commitment to finding a relationship is to enlist the aid of a "partner" or "support person," someone who is also committed to seeing you reach your goal. It can be a man or a woman, a single friend, a married friend, or a relative.

Being able to talk to this person when you feel discouraged and just knowing she or he is there to support you will make your project a lot easier and help ensure its success.

The ideal partner is another woman who is also looking for a relationship. If you know several women with this project, you may even want to form a support group. Many people who have taken "Connecting" report that the support they received from the other participants was one of the most valuable aspects of the course. A lot of them formed groups to keep the reinforcement going after the seminar ended.

Now they can say, "I went to a party and talked to five men," and not have to hear, "How could you do that? I'd never do that." Instead, their support partners say, "How did you do it? I want to be able to do it too."

Your support partner must be someone who will be able to get tough with you if that's what's needed. If you say, "I'm too busy to go out," she or he should say, "I don't want to hear any excuses — do you want a relationship or not?" rather than, "If you're that busy, why don't you postpone this for a few weeks?" If you form a support team, make sure every member is willing to be tough with the others in this way.

ᔕᔕ ᔕᔕ ᔕᔕ

ASSIGNMENT #1:
FIND A PARTNER/SUPPORT PERSON.

1. Select someone you would like as your partner/ support person.
2. Tell her/him about your project and find out if she/he is willing to support you in reaching your goal. If the answer is no, keep asking people until you get a yes.
3. Arrange to be in touch with your partner at least once a week to report on how your project is going and to make promises about what steps you'll take during the next week. (Those steps will be spelled out in homework assignments throughout the book).

As explained in the introduction, this assignment is included in a "six-week action plan" that is outlined at the end of this book. You may carry out assignments as you read, or wait until you finish reading to begin them.

NOTE: At the end of each chapter, space is provided for your notes. Use that space to record any insights you get from the chapter that you feel will be helpful to you in your ongoing project of finding a relationship.

Besides the space for notes provided at the end of each chapter, there are exercises throughout the book that include space for you to write. Feel free to write in this book. By recording your answers to exercises and your personal notes directly into the book, you will make it more meaningful and you will get more out of reviewing it. I encourage you to make this your own personal workbook.

Notes On This Chapter:

2

Drop The Veil Of Secrecy

WANTING A RELATIONSHIP IS NOTHING TO BE ASHAMED OF, SO COME OUT OF THE CLOSET.

"I know I stayed single for good reasons, but after I turned 30, I started to feel embarrassed about it," says Linda, a successful 32 year old real estate agent. "Sometimes I think maybe there's something wrong with me because I don't have a man in my life. I know intellectually that it's okay to be alone, but I still cringe whenever I hear the words 'old maid'."

Most single women share those feelings, deep down. Some are in touch with their shame and embarrassment about being alone. A few honestly don't feel that way. But the great majority of single women have those feelings and don't admit to them.

When you are "in the closet" about wanting a relationship, you're not going to be effective at finding one.

A STIGMA WITH STAYING POWER

It is becoming more and more socially acceptable to be single. A lot of people even consider it laudable. Nobody's pointing any fingers at unmarried women, so you can relax. There's no need for you to feel shame and embarrassment in today's culture.

It sounds good, but unfortunately, it's not that simple. You see, during the forties, the fifties, and yes, even the sixties, if a woman were over 30 and not married there *was* something wrong with her, or at least most people thought so. It was just as bad if she were divorced. You were around during one or more of those decades, and you learned all about these stigmas.

Books, movies, television, and your parents taught you as a child that there was "something wrong" with women who were not married. Chances are, outdated or not, that attitude is still banging around in one of your brain cells and causing trouble.

Because you haven't come to terms with your feelings of shame and embarrassment, you cover them up. You do this by pretending that you don't want a relationship and by giving excuses for why you don't have one. "I'm too into my career," you say. "I don't have time for a man; there are no good men; I'm too picky."

THE GREAT COVER-UP

If you don't believe me, try walking into a singles bar and asking people what they're doing there. I've tried it. They told me they were there to meet friends, to unwind, or that they were just stopping by for a drink on their way home.

People in singles bars (and by the way, those inside don't refer to them as singles bars) never say they're there because they want to find relationships.

Of course not. They're too embarrassed.

I recently gave a talk to a singles group. Of course it wasn't called a singles group, it was called "Education After Dark." There were 200 people there and the talk was on "Availability."

I asked everyone to raise their hands if they were single. 200 people raised their hands. Then I asked them to raise their hands if they were looking for a relationship. Twelve people raised their hands.

What about you? If you're reading this book in a public place, are you covering up the title so no one will notice you're reading a book about how to find a man?

If you let embarrassment stop you from admitting you are looking for a relationship, you will have a difficult time doing whatever it takes to find one. It's really important to understand that there's nothing wrong with you because you don't have a relationship. There's nothing wrong with you because you want one. If it's a good idea to have a relationship, why would it be bad to want one?

You have to understand this because to the degree that you let feelings of shame and embarrassment stop you, you are going to be ineffective at finding a man.

PASSING UP OPPORTUNITIES

Take the case of Angie, a woman who took "Connecting." Before the course, she had placed an ad in the personals and received more than a dozen responses. She hadn't followed-up on any of them.

She realized after taking the seminar that because of that stigma about single people, she had been too embarrassed to call the respondents. Not only had she worried that there must be something wrong with her for *placing* a personal ad, it had occurred to her that there must be something wrong with a man who would *answer* one.

After the course she still felt embarrassed, but she refused to let it stop her. She contacted all the respondents and ended up dating several of them.

In my seminars in Seattle, everyone arrives on the first night feeling a bit uptight about being there. They expect the other participants to be a bunch of losers. When they see attractive, successful, and happy people instead, they're always surprised. It helps them realize right away that there must not be anything wrong with them, either.

ᥦ ᥦ ᥦ

EXERCISE:
"WHY I DON'T HAVE A RELATIONSHIP"

List every reason you've ever given to yourself or to others to explain why you don't have a relationship (for example, "I'm too discriminating; there aren't enough single men in this city; I just haven't met the right man yet; no one wants a woman with three kids."):

1.

2.

3.

4.

5.

6.

7.

8.

9.

10.

It should be evident to you that many of the reasons you listed are nothing more than excuses you use to avoid feeling ashamed and embarrassed.

CUT IT OUT!

No more excuses.

Do you want a relationship or do you want to be able to explain why you don't have one?

🥿 🥿 🥿

BE UP-FRONT

The big problem isn't that you feel ashamed and embarrassed; it's that you let those feelings stop you from telling people what you want. Telling people what you want is one of the most effective ways of getting what you want.

When you're looking for a car, you don't walk around the showroom checking out the new models out of the corner of your eye while pretending to look for your friend. You don't tell the salespeople you're there waiting for the bus.

When you're looking for a job, you don't go on an interview and say, "I had a half-hour before the movie started; I thought I'd stop by." You're up-front and direct. You make calls, set up appointments, tell your friends, and send out resumes.

Looking for a relationship would be no different than looking for a job, a car, an apartment, or a dentist if it weren't for the fact that you feel embarrassed about looking for a relationship.

Try being direct, up-front, and unabashed in communicating that you want a relationship. It will actually help you get over your embarrassment.

THE SOUND OF DESPERATION

Are you afraid that admitting you want a relationship will make you sound needy and desperate? Even if you know you're not desperate, are you afraid other people will think you are?

Nothing makes you sound more needy than trying to cover up that you want something. When you say, "My life is fine, I don't need a relationship," you sound defensive. When you are direct and up-front about what you want, you appear confident and self-assured. That you want a relationship does not mean you are needy or desperate, and saying you want one won't make you sound that way.

It may be uncomfortable to admit this at first because you're not used to communicating about something as personal as your desire to share your life with someone else. And because people aren't used to hearing women speak directly about this, you may shock a few of them (that's the fun part).

After some practice, you should be able to say, "I'm looking for a relationship — do you know anybody you could fix me up with?" as easily as you could say, "I'm looking for the Fruit Loops — do you know what aisle they're on?"

HOW TO HANDLE SHAME
AND EMBARRASSMENT

- Be honest with yourself. If you have these feelings, don't deny them.
- Understand that these feelings are a by-product of a societal stigma that you unwittingly accepted at one time but that no longer exists.
- Recognize that there's nothing wrong with you for being single and there's nothing wrong with you for wanting a relationship.
- Take action on "Project: Relationship." You don't have to wait for the feelings of shame and embar-

rassment to disappear before you start moving on your project. Taking action is the most effective way to dispel those feelings.

Wanting a relationship is something to be proud of!

ꕤ ꕤ ꕤ

ASSIGNMENT #2:
TELL FIVE PEOPLE YOU'RE LOOKING FOR A RELATIONSHIP.

Start making it public that you're looking. Be direct about it — remember, "acting cool" so as not to sound desperate doesn't work.

Besides helping you dispel any feelings of embarrassment and shame that are still lurking about, this assignment will help you begin establishing a network of people to support you in your project.

People who take "Connecting" are always surprised at the responses they get from doing this assignment. Their friends are usually very supportive and don't think their wanting a relationship is the least bit funny or embarrassing.

In fact, don't be surprised if people tell you they didn't realize you were looking, and there's this guy they've always wanted you to meet . . .

Notes On This Chapter:

3

Beyond Sleeping Beauty

BY POSTPONING YOUR LIFE
UNTIL YOUR PRINCE SHOWS UP,
YOU COULD BE DELAYING HIS ARRIVAL.

I recently overheard two women talking in a restaurant. One of them was telling the other that she wanted a VCR. "I've been holding off on buying it," she explained, "because I know one of these days I'm going to get involved with a man who has one."

This would be funny if it weren't so tragic. You may not be waiting to buy a VCR, but I'll bet there's something in your life that's on indefinite hold until the right man comes along.

I call it the Sleeping Beauty syndrome. The story of the enchanted princess who slept for 100 years until the prince's kiss awakened her is a great fairy tale and it makes a terrific ballet, but even Cinderella is a better role model than this classic underachiever. Still, millions of women are following her example and expecting a man to be the alarm clock that will wake them up when it's time to start living their lives.

For some, it's possessions — they're waiting to buy a VCR, a word processor, a dining room table, new dishes, or new linens. For others, it's taking a vacation, losing weight, learning to ski, being beautiful, dressing well, or getting their careers off the ground.

For the really sad cases, it's their very identity. These women are not just going without new dishes — they're postponing their happiness and self-expression. As if a man is a missing vital organ, they're waiting for one to make them feel like complete human beings.

In the fairy tale, only the prince could rouse Sleeping Beauty. But in the Sleeping Beauty syndrome you're going to have to wake yourself up.

ఈ ఈ ఈ

EXERCISE: WHAT ARE YOU WAITING FOR?

I am waiting until I have a relationship to become (for example, rich; thin; a success):

1.

2.

3.

4.

5.

I am waiting until I have a relationship to do (for example, travel; exercise; entertain):

1.

2.

3.

4.

5.

I am waiting until I have a relationship to feel (for example, happy; relaxed; fulfilled; loved; loving):

1.

2.

3.

4.

5.

I am waiting until I have a relationship to have (for example, a home; fine jewelry; furniture):

1.

2.

3.

4.

5.

A relationship should be a continuation of your life, not the point at which it begins. If you're just killing time until the prince arrives, you're not only depriving yourself of enjoyment you could be having right now, you're also making yourself much less attractive.

A life that is full of interests and accomplishments and going full speed ahead is much more appealing than one that is full of potential and at a standstill. The richer and fuller your life, the more likely it is that a man will want to join it.

ᘒᘒ ᘒᘒ ᘒᘒ

ARISE AND SHINE

When Sarah took "Connecting" last year, she was a successful advertising account executive who earned about $75,000 a year. She had always wanted to live in her own home, but she had always pictured herself living in it with her husband. She didn't want to buy a house on her own because, she reasoned, when she got married she and her husband would need a bigger one and she would only have to sell it.

After "Connecting," she went out and bought a house. Six months later she got married, and, yes, she and her husband did need a bigger home, so she sold it.

"What a waste," you say? "Wouldn't it have been better if she'd waited six more months?" Then she wouldn't have had to go to all the effort of buying and selling the first house.

That's not what Sarah says. She believes she never would have gotten married had she not bought that house. The way she sees it, taking that action to realize her dream altered her self-image in a profound way. She feels it was her new sense of self-worth and self-sufficiency that attracted her husband to her. The $10,000 she made on the sale of the first house was the frosting on the cake!

Being the kind of person who realizes her goals will not only enrich your life as a single person and make you more attractive to a man — it will also enhance your relationship with your mate.

When I was single, traveling was important enough to me that I made sure it was part of my life. I went on an overseas trip at least once a year, sometimes by myself and sometimes with friends. When I first met Tony I had recently returned from a trip to Bali and China. He later told me that one of the things that attracted him to me was my sense of adventure.

I was able to bring my enthusiasm for traveling and my penchant for planning exciting vacations to my relationship with Tony. As a result, our marriage has been greatly enhanced by the frequent trips we take together.

IT'S NOW OR NEVER

What makes you think all those things you've been waiting for are going to suddenly appear just because a man is in your life? If you're waiting until you get married to travel, did you ever stop to consider that it's going to be a lot harder to get the money together, plan the trip, and schedule time off from work when there are two of you than it is now, when you're the only one you have to worry about?

If you don't go after your goals when you're single, it's unlikely that you'll suddenly change just because you're in a relationship. In fact, saying that you'll do, be, feel, and have things when a man is in your life is often just an excuse to justify your lack of motivation to make them happen now.

Had I waited for my relationship with Tony to provide the impetus for me to start traveling, most of my trips would have been to the corner newstand to buy travel magazines. Tony enjoyed traveling before I met him, but like most people, he let excuses keep him from doing it as much as he would have liked. If I hadn't made it a part of my lifestyle before we got married, I would not only be missing out on the fun and adventure of traveling, I would be frustrated at not fulfilling this dream and disappointed in Tony and our relationship for not living up to my expectations.

⮞⮞ ⮞⮞ ⮞⮞

EXERCISE:
YOUR HOBBIES, INTERESTS, AND PASSIONS

Use the space below to list your hobbies, interests, and passions:

1.

2.

3.

4.

5.

6.

7.

8.

9.

10.

If you're waiting for a man to inspire you to take action on any of these hobbies, interests, and passions, you're not only depriving yourself of enriching experiences you could be having right now, you're also passing up some golden opportunities for meeting men who share these interests.

≥≥ ≥≥ ≥≥

"YOU'RE SUCH A PRETTY GIRL — HOW COME YOU'RE HIDING IT?"

Another area where many women do not let their lights shine is in their appearance. Some have the attitude, "What's the point of looking great if there's no man to appreciate it?" Others feel, "It's too much trouble to always look my best."

While the woman who is preoccupied with her looks is the cliché, I have found the opposite to be more often true. Most women do not exert enough energy and attention on looking their best. There are a lot of reasons why looking good should be more of a priority for these women, not the least of which is the fact that men focus a lot of energy and attention on the way women look.

That men are more concerned about how women look than vice versa is a cliché that *has* been borne out in my experiences in working with hundreds of members of both genders. Of course, there are plenty of men who aren't "into looks," but these exceptions don't disprove the rule. That most men place an emphasis on the way women look is a fact that women, especially those who are looking for relationships, should learn to deal with effectively.

Many women deal with this fact about men in counterproductive ways. On one end of the spectrum there are those who fight it: "I don't want a man who is interested in looks; if he doesn't like me without make-up, too bad; beauty is only skin deep so it doesn't matter how I look." At the other end are those who feel defeated by it: "I don't look like Bo Derek so I may as well give up."

It's true that this obsession with looks is one of the less inspiring aspects of the male psyche, but rather than complaining about this, fighting it, or feeling defeated by it, you should consider it a valuable piece of marketing research. It is "inside information" that you can use to help you achieve success in your project.

LOOKS AREN'T IMPORTANT?

You dress and make yourself up appropriately for work because you know that looks make a powerful impression in the business world. Yet you think it should be different when it comes to your social life.

You may think that looks shouldn't be important to men or you may wish they weren't, but whether you like it or not, they are. It's really no different than in your professional life. Just as "dressing for success" will help you win points at a business meeting, looking your best will increase your odds of attracting a man.

Your appearance isn't more important than what's on the inside, of course. But someone meeting you for the first time doesn't know what's on the inside. If what's on the outside is pleasing, he will be more likely to want to find out.

This is one area in which you *can* take a hint from Cinderella. She knew her rags and cinder smudge wouldn't cut it at the ball, so she got a makeover before she went out prince-hunting.

LOOKS THAT KILL

There's a lot you can do with your looks. With hair, make-up, clothes, etc. you can make them better, worse, or different than how they started out. If what you're doing with your appearance is making it worse rather than better, you are practicing "appearance sabotage."

Using your looks to "hide" or to put up barriers is a way of making yourself unavailable for relationships. Appearance sabotage comes in many shapes, colors, sizes, and styles, as these "Connecting" case studies illustrate:

- Alice was 50 pounds overweight and she looked dumpy and unattractive.

  Being overweight — even 50 pounds overweight — doesn't have to mean you're not ready to meet men. There are plenty of women who are overweight but comfortable with their size. For them, weight doesn't seem to get in the way. But many overweight women are using their extra pounds to "hide." If you're in this category you don't have to say, "I'm too fat. I won't be ready for a relationship until I lose 50 pounds." You could say, "I'm going to stop hiding behind my weight and start being as attractive as I can be right now."

- Joan was very pretty, but she dressed like a slob. Her poor grooming habits made it unpleasant to be around her.

  We don't really need to discuss this, do we?

- Jennifer's hair always looked messy. She wore no make-up and didn't shave her legs or underarms. Her attitude was, "Someone is going to have to see past the superficial level and love me for who I am."

  Devising tests and hurdles for men to go through is going to reduce your odds of finding one. There are too many other women who aren't putting up roadblocks.

"I DRESS FOR ME"

Even a woman who takes great care with her appearance

can be practicing appearance sabotage. Take Audrey, a 29 year old designer who always wore clothes on the cutting edge of fashion and large, unusual earrings. She was a walking conversation piece — you *had* to comment on the way she looked.

Men rarely approached Audrey; she was usually the one who had to make the first move. She had always assumed this was because she wasn't good looking enough — until she got some valuable feedback from the men in her "Connecting" course. They told her she seemed unapproachable because of her outrageous style of dressing. It was her clothes, not her looks, that were turning men off.

Audrey struggled with this news for awhile. Her clothing was an important form of self-expression that she didn't want to give up. She had always said,"I dress for myself, not for men." But she couldn't avoid the fact that by "dressing for herself" she was sabotaging her project to find a man.

She decided to compromise. She bought some outfits that were much less outrageous than her usual clothes but that were still within the parameters of "her style." As soon as she began dressing in this less intimidating way, more men began asking her out.

You have the right to dress however you please. But unless you work in a mirrored room, dressing for yourself is a waste. Why be so selfish? It is other people who have to look at you, so why not dress for them?

Looking nice is a gift for the people around you. When a guest comes to visit your home, you go out and buy flowers or at least straighten things up. It is with this same spirit of graciousness that you should make sure you look good for the people in your life.

ⴾⴾ ⴾⴾ ⴾⴾ

EXERCISE: HOW DO I LOOK?

Are you practicing appearance sabotage? Yes___ No___.

If you answered yes, describe how you are doing this:

Now that you have undertaken "Project: Relationship," you will have to stop doing this. It is making you less available for a relationship.

ぐ ぐ ぐ

LOOKING GOOD

If you want to meet men and you know that men prefer women who look good, it's logical that you should do what you can to look your best. By this I do not mean that you should run out and buy low-cut clothes or dye your hair blonde so you can fit *your* idea of a male fantasy. The fact that men place a lot of importance on appearance doesn't mean they all like the same kind of looks. It would be a mistake to try to make your appearance conform to what you think they want.

Everyone can be attractive. You should work toward bringing out the best in your appearance and enhancing what you have. For some men, your looks are the ideal!

It's a good idea to make sure you look your best every time you go out — even if it's just to the grocery store. You won't meet men everywhere you go, but looking your best will do wonders for making you feel good about yourself.

In "Connecting" there is a session where hair, make-up, and clothing experts come in and help the participants discover how they can make the most of their looks. You may want to consult with professionals who can help you do this.

ဆ ဆ ဆ

ASSIGNMENT #3:
DO SOMETHING NOW TO BECOME, DO, FEEL, AND HAVE WHAT YOU WANT.

Pick one item you listed in the "What are you Waiting For" exercise that you are waiting until you have a relationship to become, do, feel, and have. Plan to take action on each in the near future. (For example, if you've been waiting to "be" creative, enroll in an art class now. If you've been waiting to go to Hawaii, plan a trip).

I will become _____ by _____.
date

I will do _____ by _____.
date

I will feel _____ by _____.
date

I will have _____ by _____.
date

ASSIGNMENT #4:
DO SOMETHING "OUT OF CHARACTER."

Go somewhere or do something you wouldn't ordinarily do, something you never had the guts to do before. The more unpredictable and unlike you, the better.

I plan to _____

By _____ .
date

ASSIGNMENT #5:
DO SOMETHING ABOUT YOUR LOOKS.

If you answered yes to the question, "Are you practicing appearance sabotage?," take whatever steps are necessary to stop doing this. This might involve a physical change like a haircut or a pair of contact lenses, or it might involve a change of attitude, for example, "I'll stop hiding behind my weight."

Even if you answered no, do one thing that you feel will improve or enhance your looks.

WHAT I WILL DO TO IMPROVE MY APPEARANCE:

1. _____

2. _____

3. _____

4. _____

5. _____

Notes On This Chapter:

4

Frogs That Don't Turn Into Princes

HANGING AROUND WITH MR. WRONG WILL NOT LEAD YOU TO MR. RIGHT.

A Prince: a man with whom you could have a satisfying and lasting relationship.

A Frog: a man with whom, for one reason or another, you can't have a lasting and satisfying relationship.

For centuries, children have been captivated by the idea of a frog turning into a prince. Unfortunately, this idea is still popular among many grown women. Every once in awhile a frog will turn into a prince, but most never do. That's why it's best to stay away from frogs.

Sometimes a woman spends time with a frog because she thinks that under his unpromising exterior there beats the heart of a prince. She hopes one day that prince will emerge. Sometimes a woman knows a frog will never turn into a prince, but she spends time with him because she likes him. Hanging out with frogs is a waste of time, whatever the motivation.

PLAYING WITH THE ODDS ON YOUR SIDE

If a man has every princely quality in the book but is not available for a relationship, he is a frog. Going out with men who are unavailable will diminish your chances of ending up with a prince.

You wouldn't bet on a horse that wasn't entered in the race, but that's what you're doing when you get involved with someone who is not available. Even if there were no other reasons to avoid getting involved with unavailable men, increasing your odds of finding a mate would be reason enough.

There are degrees of availability, and you should be choosing men on the "most available" end of the spectrum. It's much better to play with the odds on your side, and the more available he is, the greater the likelihood that your relationship will succeed.

Anyone who is married is on the Extremely Unavailable end of the spectrum. So is a man in a long-term living arrangement with another woman. These men should be avoided like toads.

Men who are separated or recently divorced are not quite as unavailable as those who are married. They are often still focused on the other woman, however, and may be embroiled in legal and financial matters as well. (It isn't a hard and fast rule, but you should know that the median remarriage time for divorced men is 44 months).

Someone who is single with a nine-to-five job is more available than someone who is single but travels a lot or who is in med school. In most cases, someone who lives in another city should be classified as unavailable.

Be on guard against getting involved with men who are

not available. Be predisposed to saying, "I don't want to date you because you're not available," rather than to falling in love with a man who is married or who lives 5,000 miles away.

WORDS VS. ACTIONS

What if a man's words about his availability contradict his actions? When there's a disparity between someone's actions and his words, it's usually best to believe his actions. An excellent guideline to use to help you determine whether someone is available is how much time he is spending with you. If he swears his undying devotion but can't get together more than once every three weeks, he probably doesn't mean it.

The opposite can also be true, as my friend Sharon discovered. She was dating a man who kept telling her he didn't want to get involved: he was married to his career; he wasn't interested in a relationship; he wasn't ready for a commitment; she shouldn't get her hopes up. Despite this running dialogue, he called her every day, they saw each other almost every night, and he asked her to go on vacation with him.

Sharon, believing what he said about his unavailability, almost broke up with him. I told her I'd never seen anyone who was more available and that she should pay attention to his actions, not his words. Eventually they got married.

Sharon's case is not uncommon. A lot of men who really *do* want to get involved in permanent relationships think and say that they don't, because they are afraid of commitment. That they have fears about getting involved doesn't necessarily mean they are unavailable. After all, many of the men who are now married and thrilled about it were once just as apprehensive.

If a man says he doesn't want a relationship but his actions tell you he does, don't give up on him too soon.

Obviously, there will be a time when giving up on such a man becomes appropriate, but a lot of women make the mistake of doing this prematurely. You have to give this type of man a fair chance to get past his initial fears (we'll talk about this more in Chapter 11).

GOING NOWHERE?

You know that guy you've been seeing? The one who you realize is not really right for you but who is such a close friend? The one who's always there for you, who fulfills your sexual needs, with whom you're having a safe, secure, and convenient relationship until the prince comes along?

He may be the greatest guy in the world; he may be fulfilling a lot of your needs; but if you know it isn't going anywhere then this man isn't the prince. And if he isn't the prince, he's a frog, albeit a wonderful one.

You'll have to give up this dead-end relationship or you'll never find one that *is* going to go somewhere.

People in "Connecting" are always fighting with me about this. If you have a dead-end relationship in your life, you're probably gearing up for a heated argument right now.

" . . . But he knows I'm going out with other men."

" . . . But I've been seeing him for five years, and I've had several other relationships in between."

" . . . But he needs me as a friend."

I'm sorry. I know this is bad news, but as long as your time and attention are focused on this dead-end friendship, you're not available to connect with anyone else. You aren't going to find the prince until you give up your frog. And you can't just forego the romantic part of the relationship, you've got to give it up lock, stock, and barrel.

BREAKING UP IS HARD TO DO

No one has ever fought me on this harder than

Cynthia, a 35 year old management consultant who took one of my first "Connecting" courses. Convincing her to stop seeing Randy, the man with whom she had been having a dead-end relationship for the previous three years, was like trying to pry a life preserver away from someone who is drowning.

Cynthia was quite a bit older than Randy, and she knew she would never want to marry him, but she hated the dating scene and didn't want to face the possibility of being rejected. Randy adored her and he was always there for her. It wasn't easy, but I finally convinced her to break up with him.

As she was soon to find out, breaking up wasn't enough. Shortly after they stopped seeing each other, Randy had some problems applying to graduate school. He called her for help. She wanted to be his friend, so she agreed to get together with him to help him with his application.

You can probably guess what happened. It was late, it was so nice seeing each other again, blah blah blah . . . Anyway, they got back together.

Three months later she broke it off again. Again, he had an emergency. Again, he called her. Again, she wanted to be a friend. Again, seeing each other brought them back together.

The same cycle occurred one more time before I was finally able to convince Cynthia that she had to stop being Randy's "friend." She saw that to truly be his friend she would have to get out of his life; that by being there to bail him out of emergencies she was making it impossible for him to move on.

She had broken up with him before; this time she gave him up. The loss was very painful, but the ending was a happy one for everyone. Cynthia found the prince and married him. Randy, when he realized Cynthia really wasn't going to come back, stopped hoping she would and stopped having emergencies. He found a woman who is crazy about him. Now that they each have mates, Randy and Cynthia have a genuine friendship with each other.

Your dead-end lover will probably want to "be friends" when you tell him you want to break up. Be a true friend, and explain why this has to be done cold turkey. Tell him you'll be able to resume the friendship after you've both found other mates.

By the way, everything I've been saying applies equally if you're on the other side of a dead-end relationship — if there is a man in your life with whom you're in love and who you think is the prince, but who is not available for a permanent relationship with you. Stop hoping he'll leave his wife or change his mind, and move on. By staying with him, you're guaranteeing you will not find someone with whom you could have a truly satisfying relationship.

RISKY BUSINESS

The main reason women cling to dead-end relationships is because they're afraid of being alone. This is a risk you're just going to have to take. Your project to find a lifetime mate is going to require you to take a lot of risks, so you may as well start getting in the habit now.

If you are afraid of being alone, that's all the more reason to give up your frog. If you want to have a great relationship it's essential that you find out you can live successfully without one. By depending on a man to provide you with a sense of well-being and security, you not only place a tremendous (and unfair) burden on him, you also deprive yourself of knowing that you can be happy all by yourself.

If you're worried that when you give up this man there will be a void in your life, you should understand that a relationship is most likely to occur when there is just such a void.

If you're afraid, lean on your support person. That's what she or he is there for.

ALL MEN ARE FROGS?

So far, we've been talking about women who mistake frogs for princes. Some women do just the opposite and mistake princes for frogs. Regrettably, this practice has become quite fashionable of late.

For many women today, men have become personas non grata. These women scorn men, put them down, discriminate against them, and stereotype them, but because they feel justified in having this anti-male attitude, they don't notice that they're prejudiced.

If you heard someone say, "all black people are . . .," "all Jews are . . .," "all short people are . . .," or "all Canadians are . . .," you would be the first to pronounce her a bigot. Yet you, a card carrying member of the ACLU, toss off scathing insults prefaced by the words, "all men are . . ." without batting an eye.

If you've jumped on the man-hating bandwagon, jump off while you still can. Never mind the danger that you could become a certified bigot; never mind that your behavior is hypocritical; just consider how your prejudiced attitude toward men is affecting your goal of having a trusting, loving relationship with one of them.

If the premises of your equation are "all men are frogs" and "the prince is a man," then its logical conclusion is "the prince is a frog." If the prince is a frog, you're not going to be able to have a very satisfying relationship.

Many women feel justified in criticizing the group that they see as having victimized them for generations. But to condemn the entire male gender is to cut off your nose to spite your face. The greatest damage you do is to yourself, because the negative characterizations you attach to men become a part of the lens through which you view them, and what you see is what you'll get. If you keep looking for frogs, you'll find frogs.

Do you agree that men are "afraid of powerful women; incapable of commitment; preoccupied with sex; selfish and self-centered?" When you hold opinions or positions like these, you tend to keep interpreting what men do in the light of those opinions. You see proof everywhere that what you believe is true.

It's a vicious circle: the more you believe something, the more evidence you see of it. The more evidence you see, the more you believe it. And unless you get outside of your frame of reference, you never realize that it's your own point-of-view that's at the root of the problem.

You think it's a self-evident fact that "men are insensitive" when what is really going on is that you are interpreting the facts to see men this way. Women who have this kind of chip on their shoulders tend to get involved with those men who indeed are insensitive. That way, they can keep reinforcing their belief. Or, they catch a sensitive man doing the one insensitive thing he's done in the past decade, then quickly pronounce him "insensitive, just like all men."

ᏄᏄ ᏄᏄ ᏄᏄ

EXERCISE: "THE TROUBLE WITH MEN IS . . ."

List every negative statement that you've ever said or thought or that you've heard other women say about men. List as many as you can think of, even those you don't necessarily believe:

1.

2.

3.

4.

5.

6.

7.

8.

9.

10.

11.

12.

13.

14.

15.

16.

17.

18.

19.

20.

If you did this exercise correctly you uncovered a lot of stereotypes about men, many of which you recognize to be completely unfounded. But don't some of them really seem like objective, self-evident facts? Those are the ones to watch out for, the ones you've believed to be true.

❧ ❧ ❧

It's as if you're a lawyer who is out to prove her case. You look for all the evidence that supports your side and ignore the evidence that doesn't. You win your case by stacking up the facts that prove your point of view.

Any argument has two sides, and a good lawyer could build an equally convincing case for either. But you've been approaching your case about men as if there's only one side.

You've been building a case to prove that "men are insensitive (babies, egotistical, selfish)," but if you wanted to, you could find just as much evidence and equally convincing arguments for the opposite side.

By winning your case against men, you are losing in the area of relationships. It's difficult to have a trusting, loving relationship with someone you see as the enemy. Instead of arguing for the side that perpetuates antagonism toward men, why not start building a case to prove that they are caring and supportive?

You can't change "men" but luckily, you can arrive at the same result by changing your point of view about them.

❧ ❧ ❧

EXERCISE:
"ARE YOU READY FOR A RELATIONSHIP?"

1. I only date men who are available. Yes _____No _____.
2. I have given up my dead-end relationship. Yes __No __.
3. I am open and unprejudiced toward men. Yes__ No__.

If you answered yes to these three questions, congratulate yourself. You are ready to find a relationship.

If you answered no to any of them, you're not ready. But you could be ready, more easily than you may think.

If you've been getting involved with men on the unavailable end of the spectrum, you can start making availability a primary criterion for the men you date.

You don't have to wait until you're thrilled about the prospect of giving up your dead-end relationship to cut the ties. You could take the risk right now.

If you have a chip on your shoulder about men you don't have to say, "I won't be ready for a relationship until I go through psychoanalysis and work through my prejudices." Instead, you could say, "I'm committed to having a relationship. I'm going to stop condemning men right now, and start looking for evidence that they're okay."

ASSIGNMENT #6:
DO WHAT IS NECESSARY
TO BE READY FOR A RELATIONSHIP.

If you answered no to any of the questions in the "ARE YOU READY FOR A RELATIONSHIP?" exercise, take the necessary steps to be able to answer yes.

1. I will stop dating men who are unavailable by _____.
   <small>date</small>

2. I will give up my dead-end relationship by _____.
   <small>date</small>

3. I will start building a new case about men by _____.
   <small>date</small>

4. I will be ready for a new relationship by _____.
   <small>date</small>

ASSIGNMENT #7:
TAKE ONE ACTION THIS WEEK
TO FIND A RELATIONSHIP.

Make a promise to your support person about a specific action you will take this week to forward you in finding a relationship. For example, "I'm going to go out two times this week to places where I think I could meet someone; I'm going to a party that my girlfriend is having; I'm going to an art opening and I plan to meet three available men there."

REPEAT THIS ASSIGNMENT EACH WEEK FOR THE DURATION OF YOUR PROJECT. (YOU CAN PROMISE A DIFFERENT ACTION EACH TIME).

ASSIGNMENT #8:
SMILE AT AND SAY HELLO
TO 50 MEN THIS WEEK.

When you smile at a man, you are communicating to him that you are gracious, friendly, and approachable. Just as important, you are communicating those things to yourself. You can create magic by doing this.

I first discovered this when I was working as a waitress many years ago. The manager of the restaurant told me to start smiling at people. I protested that it would be phony to smile when I didn't feel like it. He said he didn't care if it was phony, he wanted me to smile. I didn't want to lose the job so I decided to give it a shot.

At first, I did have to fake it; my smiles were artificial. But after I received a few genuine smiles in response to my fake ones I started to actually feel happier and more friendly, and my smiles became more spontaneous. The more I smiled the better time I had, and the more genuine my smiles became.

You will probably find yourself becoming a friendlier, more open, and more cheerful person as a result of doing this exercise, but that's only a side benefit. The main reason for doing it is that when you smile at men you make it much easier for them to start conversations with you, and more of them will do so.

If you're afraid that men will think you're coming on to them, don't worry. You're a big girl and you can handle it if some poor guy mistakes your smile for a come-on. Better you should have to fend off a few frogs who approach you because they think you're interested than to miss out on meeting some possible princes because they think you're not.

The more attractive you are, the more likely it is that men will feel intimidated about approaching you. A lot of men automatically assume that a woman who is really beautiful is not available or wouldn't be interested in them. I've met quite a few gorgeous women who didn't realize that was the reason men weren't asking them out. If you're really attractive, you should increase your smiles and hellos to 75.

The way to approach this assignment is make it a game. Don't cheat. Really go for it. Don't say, "I work at Planned Parenthood — I don't see that many men." The idea here is that to reach your quota of 50 smiles and hellos within one week you're going to have to go to places where you *will* see men. Don't be surprised if, as a result of looking for them, you start to see more of them than you ever dreamed existed.

Also, don't be surprised if some outrageous things start to happen. Naomi thought of herself as a shy person. But she was as goal-oriented as she was shy. When she found herself in a hotel elevator with five men one evening, she couldn't resist an opportunity to rack up 10 percent of her weekly total in one efficient burst of friendliness.

As she walked outside, one of the men caught up with her and said, "That was so nice, you're so friendly and you have such a pretty smile — would you care to join us for dinner?" She did, and discovered these men were the manager, coach, and executives of a major league baseball team. She had a great time that evening, and one of the men is a good friend of hers to this day.

REPEAT THIS ASSIGNMENT EACH WEEK FOR THE DURATION OF YOUR PROJECT.

Notes On This Chapter:

5

Frogs That Do Turn Into Princes

BEING TOO SURE YOU KNOW "YOUR TYPE" COULD KEEP YOU FROM RECOGNIZING THE REAL THING WHEN IT COMES ALONG.

I used to think I knew what kind of men were my type: Men who were tall and athletic. Men who were self-assured and powerful. Doctors. I took pride in the fact that I always knew within the first 30 seconds of meeting a man whether or not he was my type. It turned out I was wrong.

One night, about four months after I moved to Seattle, I was sitting at Duke's Bar and Grill. There were quite a few men there, but none of them were my type. I had just finished my third Diet Pepsi, and I was ready to call it quits for the evening and go home.

Just then, a group of Sonics (Seattle's great basketball team) walked in. As they walked passed me to go upstairs, I noticed several that looked like my type.

As I sat there trying to figure out how to meet these exciting celebrities, a boring looking guy came up to me and introduced himself as Tony. *After we talked for a few minutes, he invited me to join him upstairs. I went with him for no other reason than to get closer to the basketball players.*

It turned out Tony was an executive with the team. He most definitely was not my type, but since he was my entree to the players, I stuck around.

He invited me to go with him to the final basketball game of the season followed by a banquet. I accepted, again (I admit it was callous of me) not because I was interested in him but because I wanted to meet the people he knew. I didn't want to keep leading him on, so when he took me home that night I made it clear I wasn't interested.

A couple of days later I woke up with a terrible neck ache. As I sat there in excrutiating pain, crying, unable to move — the phone rang. It was Tony.

As soon as I explained what was going on, he made an appointment for me with the team doctor. He picked me up and took me to see him, and afterward took me to lunch and got me the medicine I needed.

What could I do? I still wasn't interested in him, but I had to invite him over for dinner that evening.

He asked me out for the following evening. He was sweet and we had a nice time, but he just wasn't my type. He was too quiet and shy — not "powerful" or exciting enough.

I accepted an invitation for the next night, planning to tell him then that I didn't think we should see each other any more. But I had such a good time with him that evening that I accepted another date. After two weeks of seeing him almost every night, I was in love with him.

It took me that long to get past the superficial, external qualities that I thought I didn't like. When I got to know him better I discovered that the quietness I had interpreted as weakness was actually more potent than the kind of forceful, commanding attitude I had always equated with power.

He also had a great sense of humor but because it was subtle and I wasn't looking for it, I didn't notice it at first. He was sensitive and intelligent, but it took getting to know him to recognize and appreciate those qualities.

The more deeply I get to know Tony, the more I realize how perfect he is for me. We've been married for five years and I find I am more in love with him each day.

Like all stories about frogs and princes, this one has a moral. The moral of the story and of this chapter is YOU DON'T KNOW WHO YOUR TYPE IS AND YOU THINK YOU DO.

In fact, one of the biggest mistakes you can make in your quest for a prince is believing that you know who your type is. An even bigger mistake is being certain you know who is *not* your type. And these mistakes are compounded when you make up your mind right away.

Some women do know who their type is. They're the ones who are happily married. You keep going out with "your type" and you're not happily married. This should tell you something.

CHEMISTRY VS. COMPATIBILITY

One of the things that throws many people off is "chemistry," the positive "gut reaction" you feel toward some men right away. It's chemistry when you're immediately attracted to someone, when you have that magic feeling; when you "click" immediately. This feeling can be based on a man's looks, demeanor, occupation, dress, or something about him that you can't put your finger on. It seems spontaneous but it is often an automatic reaction that is based more on conditioning than on "being in the moment."

Normally, someone for whom you feel chemistry is someone who you consider to be your type. "Not your type" is everyone else.

I'm not putting chemistry down. It's a delightful sensation and it certainly has its place in life. Without it, a great many terrific songs would never have been written, and perfume advertisers would be out of luck. However, chemistry is simply not a reliable indicator as to whether someone will be a suitable lifetime partner.

Chemistry is about as good a means of predicting whether a relationship will succeed as the temperature is for predicting whether your AT&T stock will go up. An initial positive gut reaction doesn't mean you're going to have a good relationship with someone, just as an initial neutral or even negative reaction doesn't mean you won't.

Any connection between your initial reaction and what develops later in the relationship is usually nothing more than coincidence. If you've ever gotten involved with a man with whom you had great chemistry only to find there was nothing to keep you together after the initial buzz wore off, you know what I'm talking about.

I know this doesn't explain "love at first sight" or why your cousin Vera and her husband who do have a terrific marriage knew right away that they were meant for each other. Sometimes that does happen, it's true.

But consider this: in "Connecting" there's an assignment to interview happily married couples about their relationships. One of the things people are instructed to ask each couple about is their initial encounter. Eighty percent of those interviewed so far (that's more than a thousand people) reported they did *not* feel an immediate attraction to each other when they first met.

These are not the kind of odds you want to go against.

BEYOND CHEMICAL DEPENDENCY

For a lot of people, the addiction to relationships based on chemistry is a harder habit to break than fast food. What keeps you hooked in both cases is that it's so easy.

When you experience chemistry with a man, you like him right away. It's easy to establish a connection. Flirting feels natural; you're eager to get to know him better. All you have to do is let nature take its course, and before you know it, you're "involved."

Discovering whether someone is really your type is not as easy. There's really no way of knowing right off the bat. Like acquiring a taste for fine wine, it takes time.

The problem is that in the absence of chemistry, there's not much of an incentive to invest that time. It's a "Catch-22" — if there's no chemistry, you aren't motivated to get to know a man better, yet it's only by getting to know him better that you'll discover whether or not there is a real bond between you.

Does this mean you should avoid a man with whom you have chemistry? Absolutely not. If you feel an immediate spark with someone, by all means, get to know him better.

But you should also try to get to know men with whom you *don't* have chemistry. By giving a chance to someone who you don't think is your type, you may discover, as I did with Tony, that there is an attraction between you that is slower to build but longer lasting.

It's time to throw out your preconceived notions about what kind of man is right for you and to adopt the attitude of a researcher. A good researcher enters an experiment with a complete willingness to uncover the facts, whatever they may be. She puts aside any theories she might have lest they interfere with her ability to objectively interpret the data at hand.

When I used to go out with doctors and other men with whom I had chemistry, I was so sure they were my type that for years I failed to notice that I had never really hit it off with most of them. Had I been less blinded by my preconceived notions about my type, I would have realized sooner that I was barking up the wrong tree.

Here are a couple of tips to help you in your experimentation:

1. CONSIDER HOW YOU FEEL WHEN YOU'RE WITH HIM

Usually, when you go out with someone new you ask yourself questions like "does he like me?; is he attracted to me?; did I say the right thing?; will my friends like him?; is he good enough?; why is he wearing that ugly shirt?" You focus on your evaluations of him and ignore the important question of how you feel when you're with him.

Questions you should start asking are "do I have a good time with him?; does he bring out good qualities in me?; do I feel good about myself when I'm with him?"

You especially need to focus on how you feel when you're with a) a man who you don't think is your type, b) a man you are sure *is* your type, and c) a man you are "putting on a pedestal."

In the first two cases, you need to be careful not to let your evaluation about whether someone is or is not your type get in the way of your ability to assess what is really going on between you. Looking at how you feel when you're with him will aid you in making this assessment.

In the third case, where you are going out with someone with whom you're infatuated or have put on a pedestal, the danger is that your strong feelings for him will cloud your judgment about whether there is true compatibility. You may be so focused on how you think *he* feels about you that you fail to notice how *you* feel with him. I don't care if he's Robert Redford; if you're not having a good time with him, who cares what he thinks about you?

2. FOLLOW THE "NITA TUCKER THREE DATE RULE"

Instead of disqualifying men at the "Hello, my name is Fred" stage, reserve judgment until you've gone out with them at least three times.

Remember — I wasn't interested in Tony when I first began dating him. (It actually took me about ten dates to realize he was the prince, but I knew you wouldn't follow "the Nita Tucker Ten Date Rule" so I compromised).

Don't worry that you're going to waste your time getting to know a lot of men with whom you don't end up staying.

Getting to know people is one of the most fun and valuable things you can do. It can only enrich you; it's never a waste of time.

I'm not saying you should go out with someone again if you have an awful time with him on your first date. The three date rule applies when you go out with a man who you describe as "a nice guy, but not my type."

YOU DON'T HAVE TO SETTLE

When I tell people in "Connecting" that they should give more men more of a chance, they sometimes start yelling. They think I'm trying to tell them to compromise or to lower their standards, and they get very upset with me.

DISCLAIMER: I AM NOT TELLING YOU TO SETTLE!

I'm not saying you should have a relationship with someone to whom you're not physically attracted. I'm saying that you may not always know how attracted you are to someone right off the bat.

Maybe your mother tells you your expectations are too high. I'm not telling you that. I'm telling you they're inaccurate.

I'm telling you there's something far more exciting, romantic, spine-tingling, and satisfying than chemistry. It's when you've been with someone for five years, ten years, or forty years, and the passion is still deepening.

An attraction based on enduring qualities such as love, respect, intimacy, appreciation, understanding and communication is far more satisfying than an attraction based on chemistry, which never seems to last. "Your type" is someone with whom there is the potential for you to have a deep, substantial, loving, and lasting relationship — regardless of whether or not you feel initial chemistry.

I'm telling you to go for the gold, not for a cheap imitation.

🥿 🥿 🥿

Notes On This Chapter:

6

Glass Slippers Come In All Sizes

IF YOU'RE NOT FINDING GREAT MEN, MAYBE IT'S BECAUSE YOU DON'T KNOW HOW TO LOOK FOR THEM.

Before she took "Connecting," Deanne had the same problem that many women do: "there were no good men." A few months after she took the seminar, she called me to ask my advice on a new problem: she was in love with two wonderful men and she didn't know how to decide between them.

If you think you would prefer Deanne's second problem to her first one, this chapter is for you.

First, let's try an experiment:

👞 👞 👞

EXERCISE: WHAT I HAVE TO OFFER

List the special qualities that you bring to a relationship, the reasons why someone would or should want you as a mate:

1.

2.

3.

4.

5.

6.

7.

8.

9.

10.

In listing the qualities you have to offer, did you list any of these: sincere, good sense of humor, fun, warm, compassionate, sensitive, affectionate, like to learn new things, adventurous?

I thought so.

And I bet you didn't say a single word about the color of your hair or the size of your breasts.

No one ever does.

That's because we know what's important. What we value in ourselves are the deeper, more meaningful qualities that make us worthwhile people.

But most of us have a double standard. When it comes to

looking for men, we're not looking for the qualities on our list. We're applying much more superficial screening criteria than those by which we want to be evaluated.

We're looking at what kind of job they have and what kind of car they drive. We're looking at how tall they are and what they're wearing.

                                       ⮞ ⮞ ⮞

WHERE THE MEN ARE

This was brought home to me at a 4th of July party I attended a couple of years ago. It was a weekend party at the host's beautiful island home. There were quite a few single men there as well as single women.

On the first day, I was sitting around talking with some of the single women. They were discussing how disappointed they were that "there were no men there."

"I noticed quite a few single men," I said.

"Yes, but they're all engineers," they responded. "You know engineers."

"No, I don't know engineers," I said. "Maybe you should give these guys more of a chance."

But no, the men were engineers, they were boring, they didn't know how to dress, they weren't good looking enough.

These women may not have wanted to find out more about the men at the party, but I did. I struck up conversations with all of them.

One had traveled all over the world skiing, and when he talked about his love for nature and his commitment to challenging himself, I was enthralled.

Another told me about a water-powered device he'd invented, and it was the most lucid scientific explanation I had ever heard. This man's hobby was designing and building houses.

Another of the engineers was a pilot who also collected planes and helicopters. Another trained race horses. In other words, this was an amazing group of men.

Naturally, I reported back about these "finds." I admit I had to revise my first impression of the women — they weren't as dumb as I thought. Once they realized the men were worthwhile, they started chasing them.

But if I hadn't been there to help them get beyond their first impressions, those women would still be saying, "It was a beautiful island, a lovely home, a nice party. But there were no men there."

STAR SEARCH

The main reason why so many women complain that "there are no good men" is because they are only looking for men who fit their preconceived notions of their "type." The women at the party did not consider engineers their type, so for them, there were no men at the party. They were making the same mistake you do when you make up your mind too quickly to disqualify a man based on what you think your type is.

Many women look only at "stars," the men who seem the most appealing on the outside. The rest, they ignore. But because a large number of people are competing for a small number of stars, the odds of connecting with such a person are not great.

When Meryl Streep walks down the street today, everyone wants her autograph. Any agent in Hollywood would love to represent her. But there was a time when Meryl walked down the street and no one noticed her. There was a time when she couldn't get agents to return her calls, when she went on auditions, and when she didn't get the parts.

She looked the same then and she had the same acting ability, but she was undiscovered. People ignored her then. Now that she's a star everyone wants her, but now they can't get near her.

Instead of going after established stars, I recommend you become a talent scout, looking to discover and launch new ones. It's not only more effective, it's a lot more fun.

HOW TO MAKE SOMEONE A STAR

One of the secrets of making someone a star is revealed by a phenomenon that I've observed time and time again: You can take a man who is average looking and not particularly glamorous, and when you get him into a loving, supportive relationship he begins to blossom. People who are satisfied, nurtured, and loved seem to develop an inner glow that makes them irresistible.

It's true of Tony, my husband. I'm always hearing people say how gorgeous he is. When we walk into a room, women stare at him. When my single friends meet him they say, "I want one exactly like him."

Before, the same people passed him by (I did too at first, remember?). At his high school reunion a woman came up to me and said, "That's not the man I went to high school with." It wasn't that he was unattractive before. He just didn't stand out; he didn't shine. He wasn't the star he is now.

Remember this the next time you go to a party. Instead of trying to figure out how to meet the three best looking or most successful men there, the ones who are the center of attention — take a good look at the other 12 men who are standing around with no one to talk to.

There may be four among them with whom you wouldn't want to be caught dead. Okay, forget them. But that still leaves eight, and one of them could be a genuine undiscovered star, waiting only for your affection and attention to transform him into a William Hurt, a Harrison Ford or a Michael Douglas. Remember, before they were gorgeous, exciting, and sexy stars, they were just faces in the crowd.

If you think I'm talking about "settling," consider again the qualities you listed in the "What I Have to Offer" exercise earlier in this chapter. You were right — those internal qualities are the ones that make you a worthwhile mate. When you look for men, don't forget about those qualities. They are not as apparent on the surface, but it is these internal features that make a relationship satisfying.

Ten years from now, you're not going to remember the tall guy with the Porsche who you wanted to meet at that party. If you're lucky, you're going to be snuggling up with that diamond in the rough you found, the man whose sense of humor, warmth, and understanding have kept you in love with him for the last ten years.

SCREENING — ONCE UPON A TIME

It should be pretty clear by now that you've been using ineffective screening techniques to decide which men you do and don't want to go out with. It's useful to understand where those screening techniques came from. For the most part, they're a throwback to a time when relationships served a different purpose than they do now.

Back in the cavewomen days, it made sense to consider what kind of job a guy had (what his pecking order was in the tribe) or how tall he was (more physical strength meant a better chance of catching dinner) before settling down with him.

Back then, men and women got together for purely functional reasons: men needed women to raise the kids and take care of the cave; women needed men to provide food and protection. No one talked sensitivity. You didn't expect roses or stimulating conversation when he got home from work — a wild boar was enough.

It wasn't until many centuries later that emotional factors began to play a part in mate selection. By the time our parents and grandparents were getting together, psychological considerations for choosing a mate had become quite significant. But they were still greatly overshadowed by more functional concerns.

Women didn't work, so a man's earning potential was of enormous relevance. Of less relevance was the potential for intimacy and friendship. Those, you got from your family and from friends in the neighborhood. You didn't expect your husband to be your best pal.

Then came women's lib, the pill, the sexual revolution, etc. and there were all those changes in women's (and men's) lifestyles. One result of those changes is that at least for upscale, urban men and women, the emphasis on emotional factors has greatly escalated and the functional reasons for mating have hit an all time low.

You earn your own living now, so you don't need a man to pay the bills. But you come home to an empty apartment, so you need someone with whom you can share the sense of intimacy and connectedness that family and community once provided.

This is the first time in history that psychological reasons for mating are more important than functional reasons. The shift happened all of a sudden, really. No one was prepared. You certainly weren't — you didn't even know about it. It's no wonder everyone is so confused about relationships.

Your screening techniques haven't yet caught up with your new circumstances. You're looking for a partner for different reasons than your mother and grandmother did, but to a great extent, you're still applying the same selection criteria that they used. You're still focusing more on the external qualities that were important when relationships were based on functional needs.

Now that you know this, you can see why it's important to bring your screening techniques in step with the times. You will be more effective at finding a prince if you pay attention to the internal qualities that are of primary importance in the kind of relationship you're looking for, one that is based on psychological needs.

SCREENING IN THE MODERN WORLD

The trick is to stop being so good at screening men out and to get better at screening them in. You can do this by shortening your "no" list, that unwritten and barely conscious set of rules and guidelines you use to disqualify men at the initial encounter stage.

Some of the items on your list make sense, but a lot more of them are criteria you inherited from family and friends without really giving much thought to whether or not they apply to your current situation.

Here are some examples of typical "no" list items:

• "I never date men who are younger than I am."

Why not? I know a lot of women who have terrific relationships with men who are five or even ten years younger than they are. What stereotypes have you accepted about younger men? Can you reserve judgement on them until you've had some personal experiences on which to base your opinions?

• "I don't date anyone I work with."

When you think about it, this widely accepted piece of conventional wisdom is really a ridiculous taboo. When you were in school you never said, "I don't date boys who are in the same class as I am." Why should it be different with men you meet at work? Some of the best relationships I know of are couples who met at work. That they were friends and colleagues before they got romantically involved was a big plus.

• "I don't like men with beards (men who wear polyester, etc.)."

You can't easily change (nor should you try to) someone's personality, deeply held convictions, or character. But instead of finding out about these important and permanent features, we focus on factors like whether they have a beard or how they dress. Not only are these superficial characteristics the easiest ones to change (he'd probably shave his beard if you really wanted him to, and he'd love it if you helped him pick out his clothes), they don't have a lot to do with his ability to provide the emotional qualities you need in your mate.

- "I wouldn't get involved with a man who made less money than I do."

This criterion is a direct throwback to the days when our screening techniques were based on functional reasons for mating. The desire for a man with a higher income than yours has a lot more to do with our culture's bias and your concern with "what people will think" than it does with the quality of the relationship you could have with this man.

The longer your "no" list, the fewer men you will get to know, so you should try to pare this list way down. I'm not saying you shouldn't be discriminating, I'm just saying you should wait a little longer to exercise discrimination. The time to disqualify most men is *after* you've gotten to know them well enough to determine they're not right for you, not before.

The prince knew he would recognize Cinderella by the size of her foot. When he went out looking for his woman, the screening device he used was a single glass shoe. You don't know by what criterion you will recognize your prince. When you go out looking for him, you should bring a supply of glass shoes in all sizes and styles, just in case.

ॐ ॐ ॐ

EXERCISE: UNCOVERING YOUR "NO" LIST

Part one: List all the criteria you use to screen men out (for example, "I wouldn't date a man who is an engineer; who is shorter than I am; who smokes; who is bald; whose nationality is different from mine; who didn't go to college"). List every item that comes to mind:

1.

2.

3.

4.

5.

6.

7.

8.

9.

10.

11.

12.

13.

14.

15.

16.

17.

18.

19.

20.

Part two. Edit your "no list" by going over it and crossing out every item you would be willing to eliminate as a criterion for disqualifying men. I'm not advocating you throw out your entire list. Some of the criteria you're using to screen men out at the initial encounter stage are appropriate.

The object is to end up with a short "no" list that includes only legitimate screening criteria, features that would make a man unacceptable as a mate. This is a personal and individual matter; ask yourself what really matters to you. Examples of characteristics that might be unacceptable for some women are "substance abuser; poor hygiene; not my nationality or religion; barks at the moon."

Congratulations. With your new, improved "no" list, you'll be opening up to a whole new world of men!

⮞ ⮞ ⮞

ASSIGNMENT #9:
MEET TWO NEW MEN THIS WEEK.

Meeting someone isn't saying,"Hi, my name is ___, what's yours?" It is having a conversation with someone and getting to know him a little bit.

Are you unsure where to go to meet people? At the end of this chapter there is a list of places where women who have taken "Connecting" have had good luck meeting men.

Do you consider yourself too shy to do this assignment?

Dozens of extremely shy people who have taken "Connecting" have managed to get up the guts to do it. Going out with a girlfriend may make it easier for you.

A word of caution: When you go out with a girlfriend to meet men, it's important that you make it clear that this outing is part of your project. Make sure she supports your goal of meeting men (it's ideal if she's also looking). Avoid going out with any more than one friend; a pack of women tends to intimidate even the bravest of men.

If you can handle it, it's best to go out by yourself. That way, there won't be anyone to cramp your style. You won't be self conscious about what your friends are thinking or worried that they'll tease you about flirting. You can make mistakes and no one will know but you.

A word about bars: Many women think the only men in bars are heavy drinkers. This is not necessarily true — it depends on the bar. If you haven't been to any lately, you might be surprised at the number of soft drinks and bottled waters being consumed in many of them. You may have to do some research to find out which bars in your city are frequented by the kind of men you'd like to meet.

When you go to a bar (or anywhere else), don't forget to be up-front with people about what you're doing there. I remember being asked on several occasions, "What's an intelligent and good looking woman like you doing in a bar? I would answer, "I'm here to meet someone" or "I'm here to fall in love with someone, what are you doing here?"

REPEAT THIS HOMEWORK ASSIGNMENT EACH WEEK FOR THE DURATION OF YOUR PROJECT.

Notes On This Chapter:

PLACES TO MEET MEN

ATTEND SPORTING EVENTS:
- golf tournaments
- tennis matches
- basketball, baseball, or football games

PARTICIPATE IN SPORTS:
- softball
- volleyball
- aerobics or health club
- triathalon training club
- sailing or windsurfing
- jogging club
- self defense (class)
- skiing, especially with an organized ski club
- horseback riding
- bicycling club
- hiking or mountaineering club
- swimming or scuba diving
- river rafting

TAKE A COURSE:
- coast guard sponsored boating class
- art appreciation
- fly fishing
- investments
- carpentry
- painting
- photography

SHOP IN:
- grocery stores, especially on "Singles' Nights"
- mens' stores
- bookstores
- sporting goods stores
- computer stores

- camera shops
- hardware stores
- car dealerships

ATTEND CULTURAL EVENTS:
- gallery openings
- plays, (including the discussion groups)
- museums

VOLUNTEER:
- in a hospital
- to help a political candidate
- at a public television station
- as a tour guide
- in an art museum
- to participate in a fundraising event
- to collect for a charity
- for a tournament sport by being a course marshall, ticket seller, fundraiser or organizer

HANG OUT AT:
- racetracks
- marinas (volunteer to be a deckhand for the afternoon)
- auctions

AND:
- Travel alone
- Go to bars during Happy Hour
- Join a singles' dinner group
- Eat breakfast out alone or near business places
- Visit the zoo (many single parents with kids are there)
- Take a ferry ride
- Walk your dog
- Take your niece or nephew to the park
- Teach a class or workshop
- Go to trade shows
- Join a choir or singing group

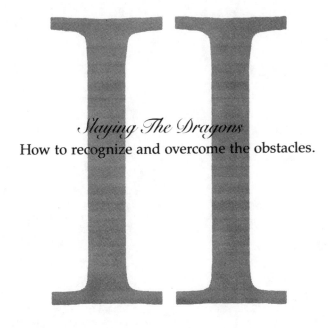

Slaying The Dragons
How to recognize and overcome the obstacles.

7

Break The Curse

CLOSE ENCOUNTERS OF THE WRONG KIND MAY BE
KEEPING YOU FROM FINDING THE RIGHT KIND.

Marriage can be a vehicle for the most uplifting and
beautiful qualities human beings can experience — love,
inspiration, nurturing support, generosity, harmony, compassion. But in the wrong hands, marriage can be an arena
for criticism, hatred, blame, resentment, abuse, and vio-
lence.

Most relationships are somewhere in between these two
extremes, but a lot of them seem to be less a bed of roses and
more a can of worms. Anyone who has seen the latter kind
of marriage close-up could easily develop a bad attitude
toward the whole institution.

Like everyone else, you based most of your attitudes and
decisions about relationships on those you observed first-
hand as a child. And let's face it — for the most part your
parents, neighbors, and relatives weren't the best role models for how to have inspiring relationships.

It wasn't entirely their fault. Things were different then. To a large degree, people chose their mates for those functional reasons we talked about in the last chapter. They often stayed together because of survival needs and cultural pressures. The strong taboo against divorce kept many marriages going long after the spirit had departed.

The collection of bad attitudes with which you came away from these relationships is like a curse that has followed you through life, undermining your ability to have harmonious and lasting partnerships with men. By becoming aware of the attitudes and fears at the root of your unsuccessful relationships, you can break this curse.

HOUSEHOLD WORDS

You didn't have to grow up on the set of "Who's Afraid of Virginia Woolf" to end up with negative attitudes about relationships. Even in a happy home, there were ample opportunities for an impressionable child to learn about the darker side of male and female bonding.

For example, unless your parents were Ozzie and Harriet, they probably had a fight or two in your presence. That was all it might have taken for you to form an attitude like "relationships are full of struggle."

Did your mother have to answer to your father about spending money? If so, you might have concluded that, "In marriage, women are subservient."

Were you ever instructed, "Don't tell your father (or your mother . . . ? That could have given you the idea that deception is an ingredient of male/female relationships.

Did your father ever have a tough day and take it out on your mother (or vice versa)? Did either of them ever complain about the other's sexual inadequacies? More input to add to your bad attitude data base.

Almost all children figured out at one point or another that "marriage causes pain." For many, this resulted in a fear of closeness and intimacy.

As a child you not only observed what your parents said and did, you also took to heart what they believed about men and women. Many of their views about relationships were dictated by their culture, the one in which people mated for functional reasons. You learned the rules of the game from them but when the game changed, you never went back and revised all those outdated rules.

OLDER AND WISER?

Becoming a mature, rational adult didn't stop you from adding to your list of negative opinions and decisions. What about that friend of yours who got involved with that overly possessive man and then never went skiing with you again?" You may have thought, "A relationship means the end of freedom." If so, that observation probably got entered into your data base.

Each time you had a relationship of your own and experienced emotions like frustration, anger, jealousy, and loss, you racked up dozens of new negative opinions.

If you went through a divorce, we're talking exponential increases. Decisions like, "I'll never get involved with another lawyer (accountant, psychiatrist, salesman)" or "I'm never going to let myself be that vulnerable again" are par for the course. It's a good bet that you were also left with a sense of failure and disillusionment that stayed with you long after the divorce papers were signed.

Of course, you've also seen and experienced the good in relationships. You wouldn't be reading this book if you didn't recognize the potential they offer for joy and satisfaction. But your positive views about marriage are not of concern in this chapter (they will be in a later one) because they are not the attitudes that are causing you to undermine your relationships.

⮞ ⮞ ⮞

EXERCISE: ATTITUDE EXPOSÉ

From your observation, what were your mother's negative attitudes and rules about men, women, and marriage? (for example, "a woman is a failure unless she's married; you have to get permission to spend money; you need to manipulate men to get what you want; the man should make more money than the woman"):

1.

2.

3.

4.

5.

6.

7.

8.

9.

10.

From your observation, what were your father's negative attitudes and rules about men, women, and marriage? (for example, "it's more fun to be with the guys; men have to provide for women; marriage is a yoke; women should take care of the house and kids"):

1.

2.

3.

4.

5.

6.

7.

8.

9.

10.

Describe your own negative attitudes and rules about men, women, and marriage (for example, "I always have to put him first; once he marries me, he will start to resent me; women are stronger and smarter than men"):

1.

2.

3.

4.

5.

6.

7.

8.

9.

10.

What do you fear you would have to give up if you got married? (for example, "freedom and independence; my friends; passion; I would have to compromise; I would have to change my lifestyle"):

1.

2.

3.

4.

5.

6.

7.

8.

9.

10.

That you have these attitudes and fears is not an indication that there is anything wrong with you. A well-stocked inventory of negative attitudes about relationships seems to be standard equipment for everyone who was raised by parents. No one I've ever met has made it to adulthood without compiling an exhaustive list.

Now that you've begun looking for them, you may find that more negative attitudes will begin to surface. If any do, add them to your lists. The idea is to get these attitudes out in the open. Only when you are aware of them can you stop them from affecting your behavior.

                                        ☙ ☙ ☙

WHEN A CHOICE ISN'T A CHOICE

Women of past generations often put up with unhappy relationships because they lacked the financial independence that would have made other alternatives practical. Partly in reaction to your observations about these women, you took the necessary steps to become independent and capable of surviving on your own. You made sure you *did* have a choice.

But a choice means you have the power to select from more than one option. To the extent that the attitudes on your lists are dictating your behavior, they are rendering you incapable of making real choices. If your behavior is controlled by the negative attitudes and decisions you've made, you're *reacting* instead of making choices. In order to exercise your power to make choices, you must break free of the hold these attitudes have on you.

Things are different for you than they were for women of past generations. Those women may have had to put up with bad relationships; you don't. Your independence opens up the possibility for you to have a relationship that really enhances your life, one that supports you to be more and do more than you could on your own.

Exposing your negative attitudes is the first step toward being able to have the kind of relationship you really want. The next step is to become aware of how these attitudes have been holding you back.

ACTIONS AND REACTIONS

We react to our negative attitudes about relationships in a variety of ways.

REACTION #1: THROWING OUT THE BABY WITH THE BATHWATER.

Nora, a vivacious and attractive 36 year old wardrobe consultant, most definitely did not want to get married. She took "Connecting" only because her mother bribed her! She avoided relationships with men, feeling she did better without them. The outward evidence supported this contention: she had a good job, close friends, lots of interests, etc. But when I began probing a little, she admitted she felt that "something was missing."

When we got to the "Attitude Exposé" exercise you just did, she discovered that because she had observed her mother leading a life that she considered boring and uneventful, Nora had always equated relationships with "selling out." She had always felt sad that her mother had sacrificed many of her dreams for the sake of her family. Nora saw that it was to avoid a similar loss of her own identity that she had chosen her solo lifestyle.

She saw that this attitude was based on past impressions and not on current reality. She realized that getting married did not mean she would have to give up everything she had worked for and live a life of sacrifice and boredom. She saw that relationships were not *inherently* stifling to women.

When your negative attitudes are sufficiently strong, they

can cause you to give up on relationships altogether. But for every woman for whom being alone is a workable choice, there are many for whom, like Nora, it is a reaction.

It's true that being alone is preferable to being in a destructive relationship. But for the vast majority of women, being in a loving, supportive relationship is better than being alone. If you want a relationship, avoiding them is not going to be a satisfactory long-term solution. Covering up or suppressing your desire will not make it disappear.

Women in this category — and you're probably not if you're reading this book — should question whether they really want to be alone or whether they're just succumbing to the hopelessness and apathy with which their negative attitudes have left them.

REACTION #2: DRIVING WITH ONE FOOT ON THE BRAKE AND ONE ON THE GAS.

Doreen wasn't bribed to take "Connecting," but she wasn't exactly there with bells on. Her attitude was,"If the right guy shows up and he doesn't smoke and he's in good shape and he likes movies, fine; but I'm not going to waste any time looking."

I pointed out the contrast between Doreen's "go for it" approach to her job as a computer saleswoman and her lack of motivation about relationships. After uncovering her negative attitudes about marriage, she realized that these were at the root of her lack of drive. They had left her with serious doubts about whether relationships were "worth it," and these doubts were at odds with her strong desire to be married.

If you're like Doreen, your positive attitudes about relationships are strong enough to keep you from falling into Reaction #1. But they are not strong enough to keep you from the dangerous "no woman's land" of ambivalence about relationships.

When one foot is on the brake and the other on the gas, you are neither going forward nor staying where you are. You want a relationship, but you don't take any responsibility for finding one. You say things like, "If the right guy shows up, then I'll get involved; it will happen when the timing is right; if it doesn't happen, it's not meant to be."

But as we've established in earlier chapters, finding a mate requires commitment, perseverance, and determined action. It is not something you can leave to chance. To take a passive role is to abdicate your choice about whether or not to have a relationship.

When Doreen saw that the attitudes and fears that were causing her to feel ambivalent about relationships were not really valid, she was no longer driven by them. When she discovered the price of her ambivalence, she took her foot off the brake, put her hands on the wheel, and started to take action toward finding a relationship. She was too high-powered and dynamic a woman to end up, as she put it, "alone by default." Aren't you?

REACTION #3: REPEATING HISTORY INSTEAD OF LEARNING FROM IT.

From her description of them, Shelley's entire family sounded like refugees from the Planet of the Apes. A recent widow when she took "Connecting," her marriage of the past 13 years had resembled those of her role models. It had been marked by friction, competitiveness, and one-upmanship.

Shelley saw that what her bad attitudes about relationships had caused her to do was to repeat history instead of learn from it. She had assumed that destructive relationships were "the way it is." She had so much evidence to prove this that at first she had trouble seeing the possibility that relationships could be any other way.

There are many women who, like Shelley, find that their partnerships with men follow the patterns established by their parents or other role models. Sometimes these women don't even try to break out of the mold because they don't realize their relationships can be better than the ones they've encountered. They think, "That's what marriage is."

You could probably make a case to prove that almost any attitude on your lists is the way relationships really are. But remember that a good lawyer can make a case for either side. If you want a satisfying relationship, you should be looking for evidence to refute rather than to prove the validity of these negative attitudes.

Even when they are convinced there *is* a better way to do it, some women find to their dismay that as they get older they take on more and more of the characteristics of their parents. Then there are those who bend over backwards to avoid repeating their parents' mistakes only to find that this, too, has its limitations. In both cases, their behavior is being dictated by reaction to negative attitudes rather than by choice.

REACTION #4: SABOTAGING YOUR RELATIONSHIPS.

One of the things your negative attitudes cause you to do is to undermine your relationships. Everyone practices relationship sabotage to one degree or another. For some people, this problem is so acute that every relationship becomes a nightmare. For others, destructive patterns are so mild they are barely noticeable.

Because it is so important to recognize *how* you sabotage relationships in order to stop doing it, the next chapter is devoted to an exploration of sabotage patterns.

🥿 🥿 🥿

NOTES ON THIS CHAPTER:

8

Pumpkins and Other Problems

IF YOU DON'T LIKE THE WAY YOUR RELATIONSHIPS HAVE BEEN TURNING OUT . . . TRY TURNING WITHIN.

Janet is a successful stockbroker who worked for the same company for twelve years. Her loyalty didn't seem to extend to her relationships, however. During that same twelve years, she lived with four different men. The relationships followed a similar pattern: in the beginning there was excitement and passion. Then they moved in together and within a few months things started to become "routine." The relationships got more and more mundane, until they finally "ran out of steam."

Irene is a 36-year-old editor who had never been married or lived with a man. She always seemed to fall for men who didn't want to make commitments. Most of her relationships crashed before they ever got off the ground.

Kristina was an engineer who wanted very much to get

married and have children. But she never met a man she could feel close to. Several men tried, but none succeeded in winning her trust and getting past her protective walls.

A string of relationships that die a slow death; a pattern of choosing men who don't want to commit; inability to experience intimacy — these sound like unrelated problems. Although these three women had very different experiences, their patterns had something in common — they were each the result of sabotage.

These women wanted to be married. But because of their negative attitudes and fears about marriage, they were unwittingly destroying their relationships. In the last chapter you uncovered many of the negative attitudes that affect the way you behave with men. By recognizing *how* you sabotage relationships, you will be able to put an end to this self-defeating practice.

The first thing to know about your pattern of sabotage is that it is hidden. That's pretty obvious, right? If you *knew* what you were doing to destroy your relationships you would have stopped doing it by now.

But your method of sabotage is not just hidden, it's cleverly disguised. It is masquerading as "what men always do," or "what keeps going wrong" or "what always happens" to your relationships.

Before they took "Connecting," Janet, Irene, and Kristina didn't see their relationship patterns as forms of sabotage. Janet thought her relationships "just didn't last." Irene knew her inability to hold onto a relationship was because men were "afraid of commitment." And Kristina thought "most men cannot be trusted."

I used to think that men were intimidated by me. It was my explanation for why those who started out powerful and exciting became insecure and dependent after I dated them for awhile. I thought I just hadn't found a man who could keep up with me. I didn't suspect that the phenomenon of all those powerful men becoming dependent had anything to do with *me*.

Then, one night, I realized that it had everything to do with me.

CONFESSIONS OF A FORMER SABOTEUR

Tony and I were having dinner one evening with my girlfriend Leslie. I had been dating him for about a month at the time, and I was eager to show him off to this friend.

During dinner, Leslie and I talked. Tony did not talk. Instead, he played with objects on the table: his spoon, his water glass, his napkin, my fingers. I tried to get him to join in the conversation, but he just acted like a jerk. I decided then and there that I could not continue seeing him: I couldn't have a relationship with a man who acted like a child in front of my friends.

By the time we were finished with dinner I was embarrassed, angry, and upset. Then, as we walked across the parking lot, it hit me — a realization so powerful that I will never forget it.

What I realized had three parts to it. The first part was an instant replay of dinner. I saw that at the beginning of the evening Tony had joined in the conversation.

I said, "Tony, tell Leslie about how you got your job with the Sonics." He told her, and when he finished I filled in the parts he had left out.

A few minutes later I said, "Tony, tell Leslie that story you told me last night." Again he told her, and again I restated what he had said, making sure to provide an insightful explanation of what the real point of the story was.

Looking back, I saw that Tony had become progressively less interested in talking as the evening wore on. I guess he figured it was inefficient for both of us to have to say what was on his mind.

I thought he was acting like a nerd because he really was one, but in the parking lot I realized that his behavior was his way of reacting to my repeated interruptions and corrections. Talk about feeling like a jerk! I couldn't stand seeing that I'd suppressed him in that way. But it was nothing compared to the horror of part two of the realization:

I saw, in a flash, that I had similarly suppressed every man I'd gone out with. I hadn't done it on purpose or even consciously, and I had done it in such a subtle way that not only had I not seen it, no one else had seen it either. But I saw it now, and the truth was inescapable — I had destroyed every relationship I'd had by inhibiting and dominating the men I had gone out with.

It didn't look like that's what I was doing. It seemed like I was "helping them improve," or "offering useful advice," or "sharing my insights." In fact, the men I dated had always said things like "you're the most perceptive woman I've ever met" or "no one knows me like you do." But my insights always pointed out their flaws and inadequacies. After a steady diet of these "insights," they would inevitably lose confidence in themselves.

My explanations for this phenomenon always cast the blame on the man: "he couldn't stand up to a powerful woman" or "he couldn't handle me because I'm too smart." In that moment in the parking lot I saw that I had spent my life looking for a man that would not become dependent, but had made it impossible for anyone not to. I realized that I had always found a way to bring men's weaknesses to the forefront.

For a moment, I hated myself. But then the third part of the realization hit:

I saw that my ability to turn men into wimps and bring out their weaknesses could be turned around, and that I could use the same power to help bring out the best in them. I saw that now I would finally be able to have a successful relationship.

This realization was a major turning point for me. Once I saw how I had been sabotaging my relationships, I could see how to stop doing it.

This realization has also been a key to my success in helping other people find satisfying relationships. Every woman with whom I have ever worked has sabotaged her relationships with men to one degree or another. None of them saw this, however, until they looked for it. In every case, discovering *how* they did this was the first step toward turning it around. They had to discover that they — not the men, not the circumstances, not luck — were responsible for how their relationships were turning out.

WARNING: DISCOVERING HOW YOU SABOTAGE RELATIONSHIPS MAY BE HAZARDOUS TO YOUR SELF-IMAGE. CONTINUE READING AT YOUR OWN RISK.

At this point people usually have four questions:

1. Do I sabotage relationships?

Do you have any sort of recurring problem, large or small, that crops up in your relationships or that causes them to end? If you do (and I have never met anyone who didn't), you should assume you are the one responsible for the problem. The reason you should assume this is not so you can feel bad or guilty about it. It's simply because by taking the position that you are responsible for it, you can stop it from recurring. In fact, the only way your pattern is going to clear up is for you to see that you are the one behind it. If the cause were "outside of your control" how could you do anything about it?

It's more comfortable to describe your problem as "what keeps going wrong" or "what men always do." Seeing yourself as the victim of failed relationships is much easier than seeing yourself as the one pulling the strings. But seeing yourself as a victim is not going to make the problem go away. It may sound like bad news that you're the one destroying your relationships, but it's really good news. If you're the one destroying them, you're the one who can stop destroying them.

It's very difficult for most people to accept that they are to blame for the way their relationships turn out because when they see what they've been doing, they feel like jerks. It's your natural instinct to avoid feeling like a jerk at all costs, so you'll probably encounter some resistance to pointing the finger at yourself.

The moment of truth when I saw how I had destroyed all

my relationships with men was an awful moment. Realizing that I had suppressed men did not make me feel proud of myself, but it was the key to my being able to start behaving differently in relationships.

You have two choices. You can consider yourself the victim of relationships or of men and continue to have the same problems you've always had, or you can view your pattern as an inside job and learn how to stop repeating it.

2. Why do I sabotage relationships?

We've already seen that one reason you destroy relationships is because of the negative attitudes and fears you uncovered in the last chapter. Undoubtedly there are many other reasons at the root of why people undermine their relationships, but fortunately, it isn't necessary for you to analyze these in order to stop doing it. It wasn't necessary for me to understand all the deep, psychological reasons behind my pattern or to figure out specifically why I suppressed men, and it hasn't been necessary for any of the women I've worked with to analyze the reasons behind their patterns.

Who cares why you've been screwing it up as long as you stop?

3. How do I sabotage relationships?

This is a key question. Finding out how you do this will allow you to stop. In the next section some of the most popular methods of relationship sabotage are described, and you will probably recognize your own pattern among them.

4. How do I stop sabotaging my relationships?

Once you admit that you do it and discover how you do it, you're ready to reform. The path to rehabilitation is also described in the next section.

NAME THAT PATTERN

Ten pattern "stereotypes" are identified in this section. One or more of them may apply to your situation. Each pattern is discussed in three parts.

1) "VICTIM'S REPORT." This is the way *you* talk about your pattern, the way you construe things before you see yourself as the one responsibile.

2) "VERDICT." Here, the "facts" of the case are presented and the "victim" is seen to be the perpetrator. This is the part you need to face in order to stop repeating the pattern. (It's also the part you're not going to like).

3) "TO REFORM" points you in the direction of change.

If your relationship pattern doesn't leap out at you as you read this section, here are two clues that may help you identify it.

Sweaty palms or squirming: If you notice yourself feeling especially uncomfortable while reading about a particular pattern, it's striking close to home.

Protesting: If you find yourself feeling especially defensive about any of these patterns, it's probably the one that applies to you.

PATTERN #1

VICTIM'S REPORT: Liking the chase.

Are you always attracted to men you can't have, the "hard to get" ones? Do you lose interest in someone once he falls for you? Are you easily bored with men? Do you hate it when they "fall all over you?"

There are several variations to the "liking the chase" pattern:

• Caroline always went after the most popular or the most unattainable guy, and whenever she "got" him, felt like she had the booby prize.

- Sophia had a string of relationships that fell apart because she always lost interest in the men after a while.
- Marcy liked men who treated her with indifference. When someone acted really nice to her she felt he was "clinging."

VERDICT: The low self-esteem pattern.

What this pattern really boils down to is a case of low self-esteem — yours. Groucho Marx used to joke, "I would never want to belong to any club that would have someone like me as a member." If you have this pattern, you wouldn't want to be in a relationship with anyone who has poor enough taste to be in love with someone like you.

If you can't love someone who loves you, you're not going to be able to have much of a relationship.

TO REFORM: Next time a man starts being appreciative and attentive, don't run away screaming and don't pronounce him a bore. Instead, see if you can bring yourself to endure this intolerable experience. Give yourself a chance to see how it feels to be liked. Notice how much you want to run away, but instead of doing so, remind yourself that it is a sign of his good taste that he likes you.

You'll be happy to know that there's a whole chapter on self-esteem coming up (Chapter 14) that will help you break through this pattern.

PATTERN #2

VICTIM'S REPORT: The passion never lasts.

Do you lose interest quickly? Do your relationships start out intense and romantic — but then the excitement always dissipates? Do you wonder how you could ever have a long-term monogamous relationship? Are you waiting for the man who can sweep you off your feet and keep you up in the clouds?

VERDICT: The parasite pattern.

You expect the relationship to turn you on, to provide the excitement that's missing in your life. You aren't responsible for making it romantic, fun, or sexy — you expect the man to do that. Instead of bringing your enthusiasm, passion, zest, and happiness to the relationship, you expect it to supply you with those qualities.

TO REFORM: Instead of expecting the man to provide the excitement and looking to see what he can do for you, look to see what *you* can do to keep the excitement alive. Janet, the stockbroker we discussed in the beginning of this chapter, tried this approach in the relationship she began right after "Connecting." This time, when things started to get mundane in her relationship, instead of complaining about the absence of excitement she made sure excitement was present. She planned a weekend trip and came up with romantic and unexpected things to do. She's still with the same man and it still sounds pretty exciting.

PATTERN #3

VICTIM'S REPORT: I give more than I get.

Do men take advantage of you? Are you always the one who "gives" in a relationship? Do you think most men are "takers?" Are you always there with patience, understanding, and kindness when they need you, but they don't treat you the same way?

VERDICT: The manipulator pattern.

Doormats say "welcome" on them, and every martyr has a persecutor. If you have this pattern you're not happy unless you're mistreated, so you manipulate men into doing just that. You could turn Santa Claus into J.R. Ewing.

To keep your man from being as good as you are, you ask him to do things for you at times when you know he can't do them. Or you ask him in such an accusing way that he has to say no. When he does try to do things for you, you don't react graciously. Instead you complain that whatever he did, it wasn't enough.

True giving is free and is done for the giver's pleasure. If you're keeping score, it's not giving.

TO REFORM: It's important for you to keep a close watch on your actions in order to resist your tendency to "give" as a means of manipulating. When you do give, don't keep score. Stop looking at what he is doing or not doing for you and when he does something nice, even something small, be sure to be appreciative.

Chapter 13 is of particular relevance to your pattern and will provide you with an effective tool for turning it around.

PATTERN #4

VICTIM'S REPORT: Men leave me for no reason.

Are you always surprised when a relationship ends? You thought it was going so well? You weren't doing anything to drive him away — didn't ask for much, didn't nag, didn't expect much, always avoided conflict?

VERDICT: The ostrich pattern.

Judy was the classic ostrich. Her last boyfriend before "Connecting" had left her suddenly, as had so many others. For her, his departure "came out of the blue." She speculated that he left her because he was going through a mid-life crisis.

What she realized in "Connecting" was that by avoiding conflict, she had not addressed any of the problems that existed in the relationship. She thought if she ignored them they would go away, but of course they didn't.

With her unwillingness to communicate about anything uncomfortable, there wasn't much to talk about. So much was avoided there was nothing left to share. Her "don't rock the boat" attitude made her relationships boring and mundane.

TO REFORM: Start noticing when you want to ignore issues that arise in your relationships. Stop letting them go by. When your discomfort threatens to keep you from communicating, remind yourself of the cost of your refusal to confront issues. Remember that your commitment to making the relationship successful is more powerful than your fears. Enlist the help of your support partner — tell her or him to insist that you communicate about whatever is going on.

PATTERN #5

VICTIM'S REPORT: I intimidate men.

Do you think men are threatened by your power? Do they tell you how insightful you are about them? Do you feel you have more to offer most men than they have to offer you? Are you supportive, always offering the men you date helpful advice? Do you tend to become their "mother"?

VERDICT: The undermining woman pattern.

This, as you may recall, was my pattern. I tried to "help" men by pointing out how they could improve and by constantly correcting them. If you have this pattern, you probably consider yourself to be very perceptive. You think you're using your insight to help the men you date, but what you're doing is constantly finding and pointing out their faults. The message they get from you, however subtle, is that they're not okay.

The men you date did much better before they got involved with you. Once they start dating you, they become dependent. They get addicted to your advice. As their self-confidence diminishes, they become less and less attractive to you.

TO REFORM: Start using your intelligence and perceptiveness to build men up instead of down. For example, when he asks you, "What do you think?," instead of giving him your brilliant answer, ask him what *he* thinks. When he tells you, don't disagree and don't offer a better solution.

At first you may have trouble trusting his answers because you're so used to your way being the best way. Don't be surprised, however, if the solutions he comes up with are better than yours. Learn to trust his decisions — after all, it was his competence and self-assurance that attracted you to him in the first place.

PATTERN # 6

VICTIM'S REPORT: I never know when it's over.

Do you stay with someone after you've determined it's a dead-end relationship? Do you feel you shouldn't give up because it might turn around? Do you think breaking up is just too much trouble (think of all the plans you'll have to cancel)? Do you justify staying with him by saying there's probably nothing better out there anyway, but do you keep having that nagging feeling that you're stuck?

VERDICT: The selling out pattern.

You *do* know when it's over, but you succumb to laziness and cowardice. You know you need to move forward, but you don't want to deal with the discomfort, inconvenience, and pain of making a transition. Instead of taking it upon yourself to correct the situation, you wait until it gets bad enough that you *have* to do something, or until an external event — a job transfer, a crisis, anything — forces you to change.

TO REFORM: If you know it's a dead-end relationship, cut the ties. You're doing yourself and him a disservice by staying together, so tell the truth about it and get out. Life is too short to settle for mediocrity.

PATTERN #7

VICTIM'S REPORT: Men don't want to commit to me.

Does all the ease and confidence you're used to feeling in your professional life fly out the window the minute you get around a man you really like? Are you "lucky at work, unlucky at love?" When you date a man you really like, do you worry about what he'll think about you? Do you not "act like yourself" around him, not say what's on your mind for fear of seeming pushy? Are you afraid he'll reject you? When you get involved in a relationship, do you get needy and clingy? Do you get intensely focused on him and on the relationship?

VERDICT: The desperate woman pattern.

You are dependent on men for your identity. (Doesn't that make you cringe?) You can probably point to your long list of accomplishments and professional successes to prove how independent you are. But underneath, you feel you need a man, that you are "nobody till somebody loves you."

If you're like most women who have this pattern, you seem anything but dependent. In fact, it is your fear of dependency that motivates you to put so much energy into your career. Your achievements are a way of compensating for the desperation you feel about being without a man.

The career you've established is worthwhile, in and of itself. But rather than solving your basic problem, it only covers it up. Basing your identity on your work and accomplishments isn't going to fill the void you feel without a man.

TO REFORM: You're so used to covering up your feelings of desperation about needing a man that just admitting you feel this way is a great step forward. Next time you notice the desperate or "clingy" feelings coming over you, see if you can observe them instead of trying to cover them up.

Don't stop achieving things, but do stop looking to your accomplishments to provide you with a sense of identity and worth. Instead, you need to discover that your worthwhile qualities are not dependent on your outward achievements. Chapter 14 will provide some tools to help you increase your self-esteem.

PATTERN #8

VICTIM'S REPORT: I fall in love with men who don't return my love.

Do you fall for men you can't have? Do you put them on pedestals and get obsessed with them? Do you have romantic fantasies about what it would be like if only they loved you back? Do you think once they love you, your life will be glorious?

VERDICT: The "avoiding reality" pattern.

You aren't in love with a man; you're in love with your image of him. You look at your fantasy lover from afar and see Superman. You think you want him to love you back, but if he did you would get close enough to discover he is only Clark Kent. It would destroy the fantasy and the relationship because your relationship is *with* the fantasy.

In lieu of a real connection between you and your dream man, you are addicted to "hope." You keep this hope alive by fantasizing. Your fear of rejection is at the root of this pattern. The fact that your fantasy man doesn't love you isn't a real rejection, because you think if he really *knew* you, he *would* love you.

You may complain that unrequited love is painful, but it's a romantic pain. It's much loftier than the pain that occurs when you deal with the problems of a real relationship. It's easier to keep unrequited love passionate than it is to keep the excitement alive with a real man whose flaws aren't adorable like those of your fantasy man. Yours is the easiest kind of relationship to have — one that's never mundane and that has no conflicts.

TO REFORM: Next time you find yourself falling into an unrequited love affair, ask yourself if you would rather have a fantasy relationship or an actual one. Then face reality: if the man you're crazy about isn't asking you out, he probably isn't interested. If he isn't interested now, he's not going to suddenly *get* interested. Your hope that he will is not based in reality.

Instead of dwelling on this man, don't indulge your impulse to fantasize about him. Don't feed your tendency to get obsessed with him by keeping things around that make you think of him or by going to places where you may run into him.

To remind yourself that you need to give up a dead-end relationship in order to make room for a real one, you may want to re-read Chapter 4. Chapter 9 will help you learn how to deal with rejection.

PATTERN #9

VICTIM'S REPORT: Men can't be trusted.

Have you been burned one too many times? Lied to? Cheated on? Have you made up your mind that you're not going to let someone get close to you again unless you're sure he won't violate your trust?

VERDICT: The hard-hearted woman pattern.

Yes, you've been hurt and yes, by protecting yourself you won't get hurt again. But neither will you have a relationship. You've built a protective fortress around yourself and now, not only can't the bad guys get to you, neither can the prince. The requirement that a man prove his trustworthiness *before* you will let him get close to you keeps you unavailable for relationships.

TO REFORM: You have to be willing to risk getting hurt. In order for you to fall in love, your heart has to be open enough that it could be broken. Getting to know someone and letting him get to know you is the only way to find out if you're right for each other.

Chapter 9 will help you overcome your fear of rejection.

PATTERN #10

VICTIM'S REPORT: I always fall in love with men who aren't good for me.

Do you always get involved with Mr. Wrong? Do you wonder why you keep picking men who aren't right for you and why you stick with them?

VERDICT(S): These symptoms could describe any one of three different patterns.

1: You turn them into the wrong men.

Like women with any of the above patterns, you may think your problem is one of "being attracted to the wrong men." I used to think my problem was that I picked the wrong men. This is a catch-all excuse for anyone wanting to affix the blame on someone besides herself.

The same man who becomes a wimp when he's with an "undermining" woman could be powerful and self-assured in someone else's hands. A man who is "unwilling to commit" to a "desperate" woman might turn around and commit to someone else whose neediness is not driving him away. The same man who takes advantage of a "manipulator" might become Mr. Nice Guy with a woman who isn't forcing him into the role of "taker."

TO REFORM: If the "wrong men" you've been picking seem to improve when they get involved with someone else, your problem isn't that you pick the wrong men, it's that you *turn them into* the wrong men. If this is the case, re-read patterns 1-9 and try to identify how you do it.

2: You think love is scarce.

You think there is only one man or very few men you could possibly love, so you consider love an overriding reason to stay with someone. You think you should stick it out with him even if he doesn't treat you well or the relationship is terrible, just because you love him.

Love is one of the ingredients that is required for a successful partnership between a man and a woman. It is by no means the *only* necessary ingredient, and it does not "conquer all." It is not a good reason to stay with someone who isn't right for you.

TO REFORM: Realize that love is not scarce. This man isn't the only man you could love. You could also love someone who treats you well. Don't sell yourself short.

You may want to re-read Chapter 4 about dead-end relationships.

3: You may need help.

If you keep ending up with men who are abusive or violent, men who are alcoholics or substance abusers, or men whose behavior is self destructive or destructive to those around them, you really are picking "the wrong men."

TO REFORM: If this is the case, you may want to seek support from someone who is trained in helping people overcome this type of problem.

There are several possible reactions you could be having to the preceding descriptions of patterns: You may have clearly recognized your pattern among those described. You may see yourself in several of them. You may have some, but not all of the symptoms of a particular pattern. You may have found a pattern that has shown up in some, but not all your relationships.

For every pattern there is a range from severe to mild. One woman with an unrequited love pattern may become obsessed with men she has never even met! Another might get involved with men who love her back, but less intensely than she loves them. Same pattern — different degrees.

Remember, these are pattern "stereotypes." Stereotypes are never *exactly* like real life. If the description of a pattern doesn't fit you like a glove, don't quibble. If it has any elements that apply to your situation you will benefit from taking the position that it is a form of sabotage you are practicing. If it's close enough for discomfort, take it!

What if you don't recognize yourself in any of the patterns described? It's possible that you have a pattern that was not addressed. The next exercise will help you uncover it.

ॐ ॐ ॐ

EXERCISE: NAME YOUR PATTERN

1. Do you recognize yourself in any of the above patterns? If so, list which one(s):

Which one is predominant?

2. If not, describe your pattern. What has not worked in your past relationships? Why are you not married today?

If you have identified a pattern that is not on the preceding list, chances are you're seeing it from the "victim's" perspective. You may not be readily able to provide your own analysis of the "verdict."

Even if you're unable to see the pattern clearly or to understand exactly how you're sabotaging your relationships, what you can surely see is that you're the common link. You're the only one who was there each time a relationship failed.

Assuming responsibility when you don't see clearly *how* you are sabotaging may require a leap of faith. Once you're *willing* to see yourself as the saboteur, however, the insight as to how you do it will dawn on you.

What if you think you have no pattern? This may seem like a laudable position to be in, but it's not. Unless you can discover how you undermine your relationships, you will not be able to stop doing it. If the problems in your relationships are not caused by you, you cannot correct them.

It's in your own best interest to discover how you sabotage relationships, so I suggest you go back to the beginning of this chapter and review the material. Then re-read the descriptions of patterns 1 through 10, and see if you can find yours. If you show any of the signs of a pattern or if you are *afraid* it applies to you, assume that it is yours.

What if you see yourself in every pattern? If so, don't get nervous — you're not a hopeless case, just a bit overly analytical. Focus on reforming the pattern that gives you the most trouble.

ᘓ ᘓ ᘓ

NO QUICK FIX

Now that you've identified your pattern, you have begun the process of reformation. Don't expect to see your pattern disappear overnight. This behavior is a habit by now, so you will have to exercise discipline to make sure you don't repeat it.

Before I identified my pattern, I was unaware of my suppressive behavior toward men. Once I knew what to look for I could catch myself every time I started to behave this way, and stop myself. It took discipline at first, but soon the habit diminished in strength.

As many people with smoking or drinking habits know, tendencies toward a particular behavior pattern may never entirely disappear. You may always need to be aware of your pattern so that you don't fall into it again.

Relationships are rarely easy. If you want one, you're going to have to be willing to fight a lot of battles. Many of those battles, like this one, are going to be with yourself.

Notes On This Chapter:

9

When You're Knocked Off Your Steed

YOU CAN'T AVOID REJECTION BUT YOU CAN LEARN HOW TO HANDLE IT.

PROBLEM/FACT. On your way to finding the prince, you're going to get rejected.

There's nothing I can say, there's nothing you can do, that will keep you from getting rejected. And it may not be fair, but the more successful you are at carrying out the steps of your project, the more often you're probably going to get rejected.

There are three solutions to this problem:

SOLUTION 1. Find the first man who likes you, and stay with him for the rest of your life.

DRAWBACKS. You may not like him, and there is still a risk that he could reject you in the future.

SOLUTION 2. Put down this book, stop meeting men, and stop dating.

DRAWBACKS. You won't end up with a relationship, and

you'll miss some great chapters that are coming up.

SOLUTION 3. Learn how to deal with rejection so it does not become a deterrent to finding a relationship.

DRAWBACKS. Rejection is a drag.

Since I can't provide you with a viable way of preventing rejection, it would be nice if I could at least offer you a cure, a revolutionary new technique that makes it less painful when it does occur. But my technique for dealing with rejection is an old one:

"When you fall off the horse, get right back on again."

That you have heard this a million times doesn't make it any less profound. This is such good advice, in fact, that you're already applying it to many other areas of your life.

In your work, in sports, in any project you've ever pursued, you've come up against rejections and setbacks. In those areas in which you've been successful, rejection hasn't stopped you from taking the next step, from getting back on the horse. When it comes to men, however, it *has* stopped you.

THREE WAYS OF NOT GETTING BACK ON THE HORSE

To illustrate the most common reactions to rejection and their consequences, let's look at the hypothetical examples of three women who all had the same project — to become champion horseback riders.

All three began by scheduling time for riding practice. During their practice sessions, they all fell off their horses.

The first woman, the Quitter, fell off the fewest number of times. She would go to the stable and look over the horses that were available for riding. She would approach them hesitantly. When none of them whinnied or seemed eager to relate, she would usually decide to go home. It would take her weeks to get up the courage to go back.

The second woman, the Whiner, fell off more often because she rode a lot more often. Every time she fell, she would sit on the ground for a long time. While on the ground she would cry, and after she stopped crying she would whine. She would feel every inch of her body for bruises. She would analyze what she had done wrong and think about what she was going to do differently the next time. She would worry that maybe there was something fundamentally wrong with her that made horses throw her. She would wish that she hadn't gone riding that day.

After an extended stint on the ground, the Whiner would get up and walk back to the stable. "That was enough riding for now," she would think. Still feeling a little shaken and still noticing some pain from the fall, she would go home and wait until she felt ready to ride again because, "It takes time to heal."

Months later, after she had analyzed her fall enough to be sure she would never make the same mistake again, she felt ready. Then she would go back for another riding session and repeat the same cycle.

The third woman, the Cynic, handled falling off in a different way. At first she, too, would sit on the ground crying and feeling her body for bruises. But then she would get mad. She would get mad at the horse for throwing her, and at herself for being such a fool. She would recall things about the horse that she hadn't noticed before, and realize she should have known better than to trust him.

The Cynic's next step would be to try a different horse. After falling off quite a few horses, she began to suspect that all of them were untrustworthy. Eventually, she stopped bringing them apples and sugar. She developed a system whereby she walked them until she was sure they were trustworthy and that it would work out, and only then did she try riding them.

What happened to each of these women? The Whiner

made some progress toward her goal. After thirty years, she was a good enough rider to enter a competition. At the rate she was going, she might have become a champion rider by about her 145th birthday, but she died when she was only 94.

The Quitter made progress, too, but hers was so slow it's impossible to predict how long it would have taken her to get to her first competition. She died at the age of 88 after having ridden a total of only five times.

The Cynic never found a horse she could trust, so she gave up her goal to become a champion rider and stopped riding horses altogether. Instead, she became a famous author. Among her books were "A Horse is a Horse Unless He's A Rat" and "The Mr. Ed Syndrome: Horses that Take you for a Ride."

Do you handle rejection like the Quitter, the Whiner, or the Cynic? Or do you combine elements of all three?

THE QUITTER: TAKING IMPERSONAL REJECTION PERSONALLY

If you're like the Quitter, rejection is so devastating to you that when a man doesn't seek you out or seem interested in you, you want to retreat into your shell and go home. Now that you're putting yourself in situations where you're meeting more men, you're going to come up against this kind of rejection, the kind I call "impersonal rejection," more often.

The key to handling impersonal rejection effectively is to understand that it has nothing whatsoever to do with you.

Remember in chapter 6 where we discussed your screening criteria? Until you saw the need to screen men in instead of out, you were rejecting them for the flimsiest of offenses. A beard or lack of one, a pair of white socks, a Southern accent, the wrong occupation — any of these were sufficient grounds for disqualifying a potential prince.

You're being rejected for equally arbitrary reasons. No matter how wonderful you are, some physical characteristic that you do or don't have, what you do for a living, and how you dress are going to be enough to get you on the "no" lists of some of the men you run into. If those men are using only those superficial criteria to screen women, they'll dismiss you without a second thought.

When you know that someone didn't smile at you because of your shoes or that someone walked away from a conversation with you because you're a nurse and he's disliked nurses ever since he saw that movie when he was eleven — is it really necessary to take it personally?

In my "Connecting" courses, we do a "rejection exercise." It's simple but effective. The women go up to each man in the course and say, "I really find you attractive. I'd love to go out with you," to which the men respond by saying, "Thanks, I'm really flattered, but I'm not interested." (We do it in reverse for the men).

By the end of the exercise, the rejectees usually start to lighten up. They see how ridiculous it is to get devastated by someone who doesn't even know them. They end up being a little more willing to make overtures toward the opposite sex.

THE WHINER: TAKING TIME OUT TO RECOVER

If you're like the Whiner, congratulations. At least you're getting involved with men. But when one of them rejects you, it can take you weeks, months, or years before you'll get involved with someone else. You're going to have to shorten your recovery cycle, the time you spend on the ground after you fall.

Staying on the ground will actually slow down your recovery. You will get over a rejection much faster by taking action on your project than by focusing on your emotional wounds and analyzing what happened to try to prevent future mistakes. Moreover, the time you spend trying to "get over it" is wasted time that you could put to much better use looking for the prince.

I was rejected more times than you can imagine during the months before I met Tony. Each time, I was tempted to give up on my project. Once, I did quit. I said, "This is awful; it's not worth it; I have a great life; I don't need anyone; I'm fine on my own; I'm not going out any more." I talked my roommate into believing these arguments, and I even believed them myself for about two days.

Then, I moved the timeline ahead and saw that the probable consequence of my decision to quit was that I would live the rest of my life without a mate. I saw that it really *was* worth it to me to go through the pain of rejection if that was what it would take for me to end up in a loving relationship.

About a month later, after a particularly painful rejection, I almost quit again. I had met a man I *really* liked, and we had just spent a wonderful weekend skiing together. I thought this was "it," but he apparently didn't. Our idyllic weekend was cut short when, on Sunday afternoon, he decided to go back to his ex-girlfriend.

I was so depressed that evening that the only thing I wanted to do was crawl into bed. Instead, I managed to force myself to get out of the house and go somewhere to meet people. I got dressed, put on some make-up, and went out to a local bar.

That was the night I met Tony.

Once I met Tony, I could look back on my relationships with other men and see them from a different perspective. I could see how appropriate it was that those non-princes had dropped out of my life. In retrospect, those who had rejected me had done me a service. By eliminating themselves from my quest, they had forced me to keep looking until I found my prince.

You see, there is one essential characteristic that every woman's prince shares. That characteristic is that he's crazy about her. If a man is not crazy about you, believe me, he's not your prince.

The men who rejected me weren't crazy about me. Any man who rejects you is obviously not crazy about you. Since he's not, you're better off letting go of him. The sooner you do, the sooner you can get on with finding the real prince.

THE CYNIC: HARD-HEARTED WOMAN

While it's true that with every rejection you're getting a step closer to Mr. Right, that information will do you more harm than good if you try to use it to convince yourself that you're not hurt the next time you get rejected.

Every time you fall off a horse and get back on, you're a step closer to achieving riding mastery — but that doesn't mean falling off is easy or that it doesn't hurt.

Rejection *does* hurt, and pretending that it doesn't isn't going to help you in your project any more than wallowing in the pain will. If you handle rejection like the Cynic, you will learn less and less from your experiences instead of more and more. If you keep hardening your heart in order to avoid being hurt, you will end up unable to experience love.

One woman I knew began seeing a therapist because she was having so much difficulty in her relationships with men. The therapist told her that love couldn't get in or out because her heart was so covered over with scar tissue. I've always thought that was an apt analogy for describing what happens to women who handle rejection by closing down.

If your heart isn't open enough to be broken, it isn't open enough.

Relationships aren't designed for "playing it safe." When it's safe is when you don't care. The minute you care, it's no longer safe because you can be hurt, but it's only at that point that it's possible for you to have a meaningful relationship. After all, if you're not going to be in love, what's the point of having a relationship?

And you can't wait to open up until you're sure it's going to work out. You can't say, "I won't get close until I know he's right for me," because the only way you're going to discover whether he's right for you is by getting close.

It may seem like a paradox that to deal with rejection effectively you have to be able to bounce back from it quickly, yet to deal with it effectively you also have to be able to let your heart be broken by it. But adopting a cavalier attitude and pretending you're fine *isn't* bouncing back. You need to feel the hurt and disappointment, and then move on.

REJECTING THE REJECTION

There's one other way of handling rejection, but it's not for the faint-hearted. If you really like someone and you think he's rejecting you for the wrong reasons or that he wouldn't reject you if he knew you better, you can let him know you think he's making a mistake.

I did this with a woman whom I met when I first moved to Seattle. One day we had lunch, and I told her that I was disappointed that we hadn't become better friends because I liked her and admired her. She very tactfully let me know that she wasn't interested in becoming better friends with me. My first reaction was to feel hurt, but then I thought better of it and said, "I understand what you're saying but I think you're making a mistake. People who know me really well consider me one of the best and most valuable friends they've ever had. I don't think you realize what you're passing up."

Just the fact that I had the chutzpah to say that was enough to spark her interest in me, and we have since become best friends. Every once in awhile she'll shake her head and say, "I can't believe I almost let you get by."

Tony did much the same thing after I rejected him.

Instead of accepting that I wasn't interested, he called me back to ask me out again. When I asked him later why he did that, he said he wanted to give me a second chance to get to know him. As you know, it worked.

In a world where most people handle rejection by running off with their tails between their legs, telling a man, "You're passing up gold here; you really ought to give me another chance," is almost sure to blow his mind. At the very least, he's going to think twice. Seeing that you have that much self-esteem could be just what it takes to make him want to find out "who is this person?"

Besides, what have you got to lose? He's already rejected you!

ON ASKING MEN OUT

What about making the first move? If you meet someone you like, I encourage you to let him know that you think he's attractive and that you would like to get to know him better. A lot of women are terrified of doing this. After all, he might not be interested, and they could get rejected.

I've never seen anyone more resistant to the idea of approaching a man than Kathleen, a legal secretary who took "Connecting" last year. A lot of men asked her on dates and she usually accepted their invitations. But she always felt like she was "settling" because she wasn't really interested in or attracted to any of the men she dated.

The one man to whom she was attracted didn't seem to notice her. He went to her gym and she saw him all the time, but they had never made contact. I suggested she go up to him and tell him she was interested. The very idea was enough to send her into a cold sweat.

I tried to get her to "role play" with me, to practice saying, "I find you very attractive and I would like to go out with you." It took half an hour just to get her to say those words to *me*, she was so terrified. I finally got her to see that this fear of rejection was going to keep her from finding Mr. Right.

She saw that if she continued letting her shyness stop her from approaching men she would probably succeed in avoiding rejection, but that this would be likely to cost her a relationship. She decided instead to change her ways. She went up to the man at her gym and managed to let him know she was interested in him. He did not reject her. In fact, he was very interested. They are now living together.

But what if he had rejected her? She would have felt disappointed; but she would also have felt justifiably proud of herself for having had the courage to approach him. And she could have taken pleasure in knowing that she had made his day.

A caveat: while I encourage you to let men know you're interested, I don't advise you to ask them out. Women asking men out is one of those ideas that sounds great in theory, but that doesn't seem to work in practice. That's the only reason I'm advising you against doing it.

There are exceptions, of course; but I've observed time and time again that when the woman pursues the man, the relationship doesn't seem to get off to a good start. Perhaps this approach doesn't fly because we're too conditioned by the long-standing tradition that it is not proper etiquette; perhaps there is a more cosmic explanation. Whatever the reason, why fight it? Just let him know you're interested and if he is too, he will ask you out.

ยง ยง ยง

ASSIGNMENT #10:
TELL A MAN YOU FIND HIM ATTRACTIVE.

You knew this was coming, didn't you? There's probably someone on whom you already have your eye, but if not, you're bound to spot at least one attractive man during one of your "outings."

Women often think they're letting a man know they find him attractive by using "body language." A much clearer language to use is English. Don't assume a man will be able to decipher your non-verbal signals or innuendos. Let him know you're interested by coming out and saying it directly.

Remember, you've got nothing to lose. If he rejects you, it's one more rejection out of the way. And at least you'll be able to make someone's day which is always a fun thing to do.

I know you've got the guts to do this! If you're really nervous about it, try "role playing" with your support person.

ເຊ ເຊ ເຊ

Notes On This Chapter:

10

Things Your Fairy Godmother Never Told You

WHEN "GOING ALL THE WAY" GETS IN THE WAY .

Sex. Never has so small a word caused so much trouble. It causes trouble for almost every type of human being, but it seems to cause the most trouble for single women.

This has been especially true in the years since the so-called "sexual revolution." Women have spent those years learning the hard way that every choice has a consequence and that nothing, not even freedom, is free.

No generation of women has ever had the sexual choices that this generation does, so there is a shortage of role models who really know the ropes. With no one to guide them, single women have had to chart their own course through the confusing maze of options. Most have found it rough going and few have come through unscathed. Many are still lost within the maze.

I have worked with hundreds of women who have come through this sexual self-discovery process, and from their collective experiences and my own, I have been able to extract some useful guidelines. Most of the women I've worked with on the subject of sex have had to learn from their own mistakes. Now others can learn from their experiences and perhaps avoid some of those mistakes.

FIRST, A FEW DISCLAIMERS

I would not be so foolish as to try to tackle a subject as complex as "sex and the modern single woman" in a chapter of a book. This chapter does not reveal everything you ever wanted to know about sex. It deals with sex only insofar as it affects your project of finding a relationship, and it deals only with emotional aspects of sex.

It does not address *health* concerns regarding sex. AIDS and other sexually transmitted diseases have dealt a deadly blow to the sexual revolution, providing women with compelling new reasons to avoid sexual encounters. AIDS is forcing many women to reconsider where they stand about casual sex, promiscuity, commitment, and monogamy. This chapter will provide additional food for thought on these subjects.

This chapter also does not address *moral* concerns. While I have the utmost respect for religious convictions that may influence a woman's choices about having or not having sex, morality is not my field.

These moral and health considerations are certainly of as much, if not greater, import than the emotional concerns with which we will be dealing. While I am making a separation between these concerns and the emotional ones on which we will be focusing, I encourage you to take all these factors into account in choosing whether, when, and with whom to have sex.

The last subject we will not be addressing is "casual sex." One of the choices women have today (or had before AIDS) is to go to bed with a man "just for fun." We are not going to address those sexual encounters that are "purely recreational," the ones you know will not lead to a relationship. The following discussion is meant to apply to sexual encounters with someone with whom you *do* want to build an enduring relationship.

SEX AND RELATIONSHIPS: THE CRITICAL CONNECTION

You may have noticed that sex tends to get in the way of relationships. This chapter is about how to keep it from doing that.

When sex is most likely to have an adverse affect on a relationship is when you have it too soon. I advise women to wait much longer than they ordinarily think they need to before having sex with a man. I advise this only because it works. If having sex on the first date or at an early stage of getting to know someone forwarded women in having satisfying lifetime relationships, I would be all for it.

But by going to bed with a man too soon, you put a strain on the relationship from which it will have a hard time recovering. Getting a relationship off the ground is a fragile enough undertaking — why load it down with this unnecessary burden?

You don't cross home plate without first touching first, second, and third bases. Only after we cover the bases of emotional and psychological intimacy are we ready for the more intense physical intimacy that we experience when we have sex with someone. By jumping ahead to the physical intimacy before we've built up to it we create a gap, so to speak. We have to work backwards to fill in the psychological and emotional intimacy, and this is very difficult to do.

This gap is one of the things that gives rise to the awkwardness of "the morning after" and the phenomenon of one of you (usually the man) running away after an initial sexual encounter. The disparity between the enormous degree of physical intimacy you've experienced and the relatively small degree of psychological and emotional closeness that exists between you makes you feel uncomfortable. You don't know how to go about bridging that gap, so one of you bolts.

You get yourself into this situation when you don't know how to accurately gauge the degree of intimacy that exists between the two of you before you have sex. When you spend a wonderful evening talking with a man you really like, you feel very close to him. Because you really enjoy this feeling, you want to get closer. Your desire for intimacy and the physical attraction you're feeling cloud your judgment. It "feels" right, so you go with the flow.

READY OR NOT . . .

Another reason you jump into sex is that although the intense excitement that comes with this new sense of closeness is pleasurable, it's also uncomfortable. The excitement and love and passion and closeness is a bit overwhelming, and you have sex partly to get rid of these intense feelings.

It's like getting an exciting looking present and having to leave it under the tree until Christmas. Some people enjoy that prolonged anticipation, but for most of us, it's excruciating. We're impatient to open the present, but opening it before Christmas not only robs us of some of the satisfaction, it also detracts from the spirit of the holiday.

The key is learning to prolong the feelings of excitement and anticipation rather than getting rid of them by taking things to the next step right away. By patiently allowing a friendship to unfold at a natural pace, you get around to covering all the bases before you have sex. You create a more solid foundation on which to build a relationship.

FROM SEX TO LOVE:
YOU CAN'T GET THERE FROM HERE

Sandra is a 31 year old woman who owns her own

clothing company. Before she took "Connecting," she used to go to bed with a man soon after they began dating. More than sex itself, she liked the intimacy she felt when she cuddled up with her lover afterward.

For Sandra, sex was a way of "feeling closer" to a man. Like many women, she tried to use it as a shortcut to love. But while sex can be an expression of love, it is not a means of achieving it any more than dining at expensive restaurants is a means of achieving wealth.

Women tend to equate sex with intimacy, love, and affection. It's true that sex can induce these feelings, but it does so in much the same way that a drug induces feelings of euphoria. This drug high wears off as soon as the physical stimulus that gave rise to it is gone. If intimacy and affection are not there *before* you have sex, they will disappear afterward.

Intimacy, love, and affection have to be earned. There is no shortcut to these feelings. Unless they are based on shared experiences and mutual understanding and appreciation, they do not have a foundation. They are like a mirage that disappears when you take a closer look.

Women with low self-esteem are especially prone to having sex as a means of experiencing love. These women may also be having sex as a way of validating their desirability. They seek to get a man's "approval" by having sex with him, but the temporary gratification always wears off, leaving emptiness in its wake.

Women who try to use sex as a shortcut to love find that it actually takes them in the opposite direction.

WILL HE STILL LOVE YOU TOMORROW?

For the majority of women, having sex is a matter of much more significance than it is for most men. This is probably due in part to biological factors and in part to centuries of conditioning. That men do not attach the same expectations to sex as do most women may not be fair, but it is nonetheless true.

When you go to bed with a man you really like, you experience a bond with him, an intense connection. You feel a commitment toward him — not necessarily a deep or permanent one, but a commitment nevertheless. You expect a relationship to develop. That's why you're so devastated when you go to bed with someone you like and he doesn't call you afterward. (The disparity between your level of commitment and his is another reason why a man may "run away" the next day).

Much of the rhetoric of the last two decades has attempted to convince us otherwise, but for most women, it's almost impossible to have sex with someone they really care about without it setting up expectations. When you have sex with a man you like, it's not a "casual fling." Like it or not, it is a significant step, one that means a lot to you.

Denying this will not help. You need to look beyond the opinions you've embraced about this issue and discover what the truth is for you. When you know what sex really means to you and what it represents to you, you can be responsible for having your actions reflect these attitudes.

When you're aware of all the implications of going to bed with someone, you can make a more informed choice about whether and when to take this step. If you discover that for you, sex really isn't such a casual thing, you'll be less likely to jump into it too soon. You'll be more likely to wait until his level of commitment catches up to yours.

How can you tell when you're ready? One indicator is that if you have the slightest question in your mind about whether a man is going to call you afterward, it's too soon. If you aren't sure whether you're ready, err on the side of waiting too long. Even if you think you *are* ready, before the eighth date is almost certainly too soon.

AFTER THE REVOLUTION

There are a variety of other reasons why women have sex too early. "I don't want him to think I'm a prude" and "He may not ask me out again if I don't" are two that are related. Some men will think you're a prude and some won't ask you out again if you don't, but these are probably the same men who won't call you again if you do.

Then there are the women who say, "I'm liberated and can have sex whenever I want." This attitude was very popular during the sixties and was probably a necessary phase for a lot of women to go through. But somebody should tell these women that the sexual revolution is over and we won. To be liberated is to be mature enough to make constructive choices that serve your best interests.

Most women today reject the external societal taboos that have traditionally kept them from having sex. But as they continue to come to grips with their sexual freedom, many of these women are coming full circle to the conviction that "waiting" may still be a good idea.

🥿 🥿 🥿

Notes On This Chapter:

11

How To Capture A Prince

CAGES AND TRAPS
WON'T HOLD A MAN'S HEART.

David, a 38 year old man who recently took "Connecting" has a problem with "women over 30." "You talk with them for a few minutes, and then the conversation stops flowing," he says. "You can hear their wheels turning as they work their way toward getting you to ask them out. They always seem like they're trying to 'close the deal'."

Richard is another man I know who has had similar experiences. He is 36 years old and he recently started to date much younger women. When I asked him why, he said, "I think women over 30 are gorgeous and I like their intelligence and independence, but I find I can't have fun with them anymore. After two or three dates they always want to talk about settling down and getting married. I want to go out with someone who's fun, not someone who is desperate to find the right genes for her baby."

At a party I attended recently, I overheard a man entertaining a crowd of people with a description of a recent blind date. According to him, before they even got to dinner she had asked him about his family's medical history, his intentions regarding marriage and children, and his future career prospects. Exaggeration or not, judging by the laughter he got from his small audience, his story struck a responsive chord.

The 30+ year old woman who is so desperate to get married and have children that she practically handcuffs every man she meets is not merely a figment of the male imagination — she actually exists. She is out there and she is dangerous. You need to find this woman and you need to stop her!

TICK TOCK

When you listen carefully, can you hear your biological clock ticking away? Do you fear that if you don't settle down soon it will be too late? Do you count the child-bearing months and years that are still ahead of you, and lament that you waited so long?

Maybe you're not worried about having children. Still, are you afraid that your odds of finding a good man are diminishing with each passing year? When you meet someone you like do you try to fit him into the role of "husband" right away? Do you read a casual remark about doing something together in the future as a sign of a lifetime commitment?

Think back to when you were twenty. You didn't have those thoughts then. You were "in the moment" with your relationships. Unencumbered with the weight of your expectations and fears, they developed naturally. When you went out with a man, you both had *fun*.

Somewhere along the way, you changed. You started thinking of time as something that was running out. You started focusing on the destination — marriage — and you stopped enjoying yourself along the way.

ARE WE THERE YET?

Rebecca was a 29 year old administrative assistant who really wanted to get married. She started dating a man named Bob, and soon decided she really liked him. He seemed to care for her, too. Things were great, they got along beautifully, etc.

After a couple of months, however, she began to feel frustrated with the way the relationship was going. She felt she and Bob were just drifting along aimlessly. She wanted to plan for the future. She wanted to know if he was serious, because if he wasn't, she didn't want to waste her time. As she put it, she wanted to "pin this thing down."

Rebecca broached the subject of marriage to Bob, who made it clear he wasn't ready to think about something that serious. Having recently gone through a divorce, he wasn't sure he ever wanted to get married again, but he was sure he didn't want to for awhile. Rebecca kept pressing this issue, and finally, Bob stopped asking her out.

Rebecca's desperate attitude toward marriage had driven away other men before Bob, and it will probably drive away many more. But even if she succeeds in pressuring a man into marrying her, her view of marriage as an "end destination" is likely to result in an unhappy relationship. I teach a course for couples, and over and over again I've observed the consequences when one or both partners enter into a marriage with the expectation that this step is the "end." They stop working to keep their relationships romantic, supportive, and exciting. They stop growing together, and their marriages became unhappy.

If you are like Rebecca, you view marriage as though it is an island toward which you are swimming. All your energy is directed toward reaching the island. You think when you get there you will finally be able to relax and stop swimming. What you don't realize is that this island is filled with water. When you get there, you'll only have to keep swimming.

When you date a man you like, you try to rush him to the island instead of enjoying the experience of swimming together. If you understood that marriage is nothing but a long swim, you wouldn't be in such a rush to get there. You could enjoy the relationship *now,* and before you knew it, you would be at your destination. After all, since you're only going to continue swimming once you get there, what's the big rush?

STOPPING THE FLOW

It's the *substance* that really matters in a relationship, both before and after marriage. Instead of appreciating the substance — the companionship, mutual support, and intimacy that are already there — you try to establish a *form,* a definition or set of boundaries. You try to put your relationship "into a box," or, in Rebecca's words, to "pin this thing down."

One reason why you try to put your relationship into a box is because of your excitement and enthusiasm about it. You're not used to these feelings, and although they are pleasurable, they make you uncomfortable. Instead of just *feeling* the excitement, you try to *do something* about it. It's not unlike what we talked about in the last chapter — having sex too soon as a way of handling the intense excitement and intimacy of a new relationship.

Another reason you try to put a relationship in a box is because you are afraid it won't unfold properly on its own. You fear that it will disappear, so you try to hold onto it.

If a relationship is good, it will unfold in its own time and its own way. Given room to breathe, it will flouirish and expand naturally. But when you try to direct how and when it develops you interfere with the natural flow of things, which is never a good idea. You suffocate the relationship and you destroy it.

OH, NO! NOT ANOTHER RISK!

What about the risk that if you don't force the issue, you'll waste your time with someone who doesn't end up marrying you? After all, you're not getting any younger.

Unfortunately, there's no way around this dilemma. If you want a relationship, you have to take the risk that you'll "waste" your time with men you don't end up marrying. The only way to find out whether a relationship will last is to get deeply involved in it, all the way to the point that it either works out or it doesn't. You just can't call these things from the outside.

(Of course, once you're *sure* that a relationship is going nowhere it is important to bail out. There's a difference between a dead-end relationship and one that's future is still unknown. A dead-end relationship is one that you *know* is not going to last, and that keeps you from being available for the prince.)

As long as a relationship is unfolding and progressing, you should stick with it and enjoy the process. It's only when you are too focused on your goal of being married that you regard friendships that don't end in marriage as a waste. A much better (and more accurate) point-of-view is that each man with whom you get involved is helping to prepare you for your relationship with the prince. I learned something from every relationship I had before I met Tony, and I don't consider any of them a waste.

Your relationships with men are not just valuable as stepping stones to the prince. They are worthwhile simply because being involved with people enriches your life. You should appreciate the experiences you have with men just for the sake of those experiences, no matter what their outcome. Letting go of your concern over "where it is going" will enable you to live your life more fully *right now.*

This doesn't mean that it is never legitimate to force the issue of marriage. There may come a time in your relationship when this will be appropriate and necessary. However, there are effective and ineffective ways of doing this. Letting go of the notion that marriage is an "end destination" that you have to get to as quickly as possible is the first step toward being able to approach this issue effectively.

The next step is to learn how to deal with a man's fear of commitment.

COMMITMENT: YOURS AND HIS

As many women have observed, many men are afraid of commitment. While this fear can arise for women too, it's true that men are much more prone to it. To understand why, you have to realize that commitment is a word that men and women define differently.

Webster's Dictionary supplies both the female definition: "to bind as by a promise; engage," and the one accepted by most men: "to put officially in custody or confinement (committed to prison)."

When you get close with a man, even one who *wants* to get married, at some point he will probably get scared and want to bolt. This reaction is predictable, a milestone you can expect to encounter on the road to establishing a relationship. Understanding that men view commitment as confinement is the first step toward dealing with them effectively about this issue.

A man's fear of commitment is reinforced whenever he encounters that woman we talked about before, the one with the handcuffs. When you're too focused on getting a man to marry you, you start putting pressure on him and you stop being fun. It's no wonder he wants to run. You would too if you thought someone was trying to put you in a cage and put an end to your enjoyment of life.

But even when he's not being pressured, a man may want to bolt. One reason for this is that many men, by the time they've reached their 30s, have been through one or several disappointing relationships. These have made them gun-shy.

A large percentage of single men are divorced, and divorced people are especially gun-shy because they tend to feel that they have failed. No matter how amicable the separation, people who have been divorced usually hold it as a failure. They don't often admit to this: "We left on good terms, we still like each other, we just weren't right for each other."

But when they got married, it was their intention to stay married "forever," not to "try it out for a few years." A divorce represents the shattering of that dream. (By the way, if you are divorced, you will more easily put it behind you by facing up to those feelings of failure rather than by covering them up and insisting you have no problem with what happened).

Whether or not a man has been through a divorce, he has probably been seriously disappointed by a relationship at one time or another, with the result that he has become wary of them. The men you date may not see their fear of commitment as an unwillingness to face failure again. But it is important for you to understand that for many of them, that's what it is.

So how do you deal with it when a man's fear of commitment rears its ugly head?

DON'T FIGHT IT

Tony and I had been going together for several months when he asked me to move in with him. I was a little unsure about making this move, but I went along with it at his insistence.

A couple of days after I moved in, we were sitting in the living room, talking. I mentioned the idea of our taking a vacation together that summer. All of a sudden I noticed his eyes begin to glaze over. He looked upset and seemed to get withdrawn.

I sensed what was happening. I asked, "Tony, are you feeling trapped? He replied, "Yes," as if in a trance.

"How dare you feel trapped," was my first angry response. "You're the one who wanted me to live here; I didn't force you into this. I can't believe you think I trapped you."

Luckily, I didn't voice those thoughts. I realized that this was just a stage Tony was going through and that it had nothing to do with me. I said, "I understand. You're feeling trapped. Is there anything you want me to do about it?" He said, "No."

Tony went through similar experiences several times during the next few months. Each time I noticed the signs, I would ask, "Are you feeling trapped right now?" He would say, "Yeah, I am," and I would say, "Oh."

I didn't ignore Tony's fear, but neither did I get angry, defend myself, or try to change the way he felt. I just let him go through "feeling trapped," and eventually he got past this stage.

Most women, when they encounter a man's fear of commitment, don't handle it this way. Instead, they take it personally and get hurt and angry, which only intensifies the problem. When a man comes up against his fear of commitment, your job should be to help him get over this hump. Fighting it, feeling bad or upset, taking it personally, condemning him, or trying to force him to stop feeling that way will only make it harder for him to get past this stage.

I shudder to think of how many women have lost men they cared about because they took it personally when a man expressed his fear of commitment. To escape from the pressure and from the guilt they felt over hurting someone they cared about, the men bolted.

FROM MARRIAGE TO COMMITMENT: YOU CAN'T GET THERE FROM HERE

Another way women react to a man's resistance to commitment is by trying to force him to commit. Forcing someone to marry you will not make him get committed if he's not. Commitment is a state of mind; it can't be generated externally. Forcing a man into an *act* of commitment before he has arrived at this state of mind does not work. Women who do this are, once again, going after the form instead of the substance.

The other side of this is women who fail to recognize it when a man *is* commited. When you think commitment must be exhibited through a particular behavior, you assume that the lack of this behavior means there is no commitment. This is another way of confusing form with substance.

A man may be committed to you and yet be afraid of marriage. Mistaking his unwillingness to get married for a lack of commitment is likely to cost you the relationship. Approaching a man who *is* committed as though he is *not* will only stifle his commitment.

While getting a man to marry you will never get him to be committed to you, if he already *is* committed, getting married may be a good idea. Left to their own devices, most men will not express their commitment by getting married. Therefore, it is often up to the women to provide the impetus for taking this step.

In working with hundreds of men, I have met very few who *wanted* to get married. I have met lots, however, who got married. Once they did, most of them loved it.

FORCE THE ISSUE, NOT THE MAN

It is appropriate to force the issue of marriage when:
a) You know marriage is not an "end" but a continuation of

the relationsip that already exists.
b) You love each other and he is committed to you.
c) You want to marry him.
d) He doesn't want to get married.

My friend Claire taught me about the art and science of forcing the issue of marriage. She was a real master at this, and it's a good thing she was, because her boyfriend, Martin, had a more severe allergy to marriage than any man I've ever met.

It was about nine years ago in San Francisco when Claire told Martin it was time to get married. They had been living together for seven years, and he would have preferred to go on that way forever. He didn't want to lose her, however; so he agreed to marry her.

They asked me to meet with them to help them plan their wedding. When I arrived at their apartment at the time we had agreed to meet, Martin wasn't home yet. Normally a punctual person, he arrived 45 minutes late.

The three of us sat down with our lists and pages of notes and started to talk about the wedding plans. Martin got up to get something from the kitchen and came back ten minutes later. We resumed the meeting. Five minutes later he left abruptly to make a phone call. This sort of thing went on for about an hour.

Finally I asked Martin what was wrong. "Nothing," he said. Claire said, "You don't want to get married, right?" There was a pause, then Martin signed and said, "No, I don't."

I thought Claire would cry or get mad or be devastated, but she just said, "I understand. What do you want to do about this?"

Martin said he wanted to go out for a walk. After he left, I turned to Claire and asked, "Does this mean the wedding's off?" She said, "No, it just means he doesn't want to get married. He never wants to go out and run either, but he does it anyway, and then he's always glad afterward. This is the same kind of thing."

I asked, "Don't you feel bad that he's not enthusiastic about marrying you?" She said, "Of course I would like it better if he were sweeping me off my feet instead of kicking and screaming over this, but he's the man I want, and this is the way he is. I can't change his attitude about marriage, so I don't try. When he talks about not wanting to do it, I don't argue with him. I just keep going forward with our plans because I know he'll get over this resistance sooner or later."

As it turned out, Martin got over his resistance later, not sooner. He had second thoughts until his wedding day. But the wedding proceeded as planned, and they have been happily married for the past eight years.

What made Claire effective in her relationship with Martin was that she recognized he *was* committed to her, and she dealt with him on that basis. She didn't take his lack of enthusiasm personally.

There is a terrific man out there who has left every woman with whom he's been involved because they each took his fear of commitment or his lack of enthusiasm about marriage personally. As soon as he meets a woman who knows how to help him get through these hurdles, he'll marry her. He could be the next man you meet . . .

꧁ ꧁ ꧁

Notes On This Chapter:

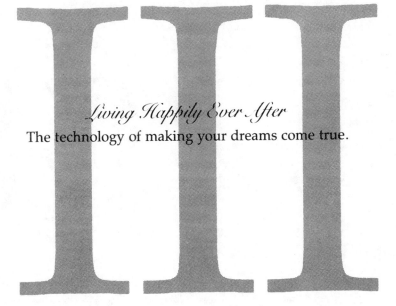

III

Living Happily Ever After

The technology of making your dreams come true.

12

Try A Little Alchemy

INTIMACY IS THE KEY THAT UNLOCKS THE TREASURE WITHIN.

The first thing a woman should do when she starts dating a man is to get intimate with him. By this I *don't* mean have sex right away, as you know from chapter 10. You should have intimacy first and sex much later — but women today tend to do just the opposite. They have sex right away, but postpone *really* getting to know someone.

You may think you are getting to know a man just because you are spending time with him. But finding out *about* someone is not the same as getting to know him.

Intimacy came easily during your high school and college years. You could meet someone at a party and be close friends by the next day. It wasn't unusual back then to stay up half the night with someone, talking about things that really mattered. And no subject was off limits.

But as you got older you became less interested in being with men just for the sake of sharing experiences. You became much more concerned with the outcome of relationships, with "where they were going."

The more relationships started to matter to you and the more you felt you had at stake in them, the less risks you were willing to take. You stopped "jumping into intimacy" with people, and to a large extent, you forgot how.

It's easier to become intimate with a man right away than it is after you've dated him for awhile. On most dates, people do things together that don't encourage them to talk. You don't get to know someone at a movie, disco, theatre, or sports event.

By limiting the quantity and quality of your conversations, you establish unspoken boundaries. The longer you wait to cross these, the harder it gets. To maximize the opportunity for intimacy, try to plan conversation-encouraging activities like walks and quiet dinners.

HOW TO GET PAST THE WRAPPING

To get intimate with a man, you have to learn how to become a good interviewer. Normally when you interview someone you've just met, you ask him what his job is, what kind of car he drives, where he likes to go skiing, what restaurants he enjoys, etc. You discuss the wrapping and never get inside the package. Questions like these help you discover whether a man fits into your lifestyle; they express your interest in *yourself,* not in him.

Later in this chapter there is a list of "ice-breaking" questions that will help you encourage a man to communicate about some of his inner thoughts and feelings. The spirit in which you ask these questions is as important as the questions themselves.

When you interview someone with the intention of getting intimate, you must be interested in *him.* If you're not intensely interested in him, pretend that you are. If you're having trouble, remember that he may be a diamond in the rough just waiting to be discovered by someone who's willing to do a little digging. Or imagine that you're writing a biography about him or that you're Barbara Walters.

The key is *listening*. You have to listen like you mean it.

Just like that time my "fake" smiles turned into genuine ones after people started reacting to them, you'll find that as people respond to your feigned curiosity about them, your interest will become genuine. You'll also find that when people are talking about what they're really thinking and feeling, they are anything but dull.

Your job is to ferret out the Superman beneath the Clark Kent in every man you meet. Your goal should be to have men say to you "I haven't been able to talk with someone like this in years."

Most people won't automatically open up to you. It takes skill to get them to reveal their deeper thoughts and feelings. As with any talent, you'll get better with practice.

By developing the ability to get intimate, you'll be helping to ensure that you don't let a potential prince slip through your fingers. When you do eliminate someone, your decision will be an informed one; you'll know who it is you're passing up. And if it doesn't work out, you'll find you were enhanced by the intimate contact you had during the time you spent together. Some of the questions on the next page may seem overly personal, especially for a first date (which is when I recommend you start springing them). I assure you, you won't offend a man by asking him these questions in the spirt of genuine interest.

I'm not saying he won't get embarrassed. I remember when I first asked Tony some of these questions, he said to me, "You're so personal, it's embarrassing." I asked him if he wanted me to stop, and he said, "No, I like it."

The truth is, people are dying for intimacy. Besides, it's a rare person who's favorite subject isn't him(or her)self. Don't be surprised if your interest in this subject makes him think *you're* fascinating!

Intimacy is a two-way street, but you'll find that revealing yourself will be much easier once you start the ball rolling with him. As he opens up, it will become more comfortable for you to do so.

Intimacy involves risks. To get to know him, you may have to ask him about personal things; you risk intruding. To let him get to know you, you have to reveal yourself; you risk rejection.

Another "risk" is that it won't work out, that you'll end up wasting your time. But it's never a waste to get to know someone deeply. The waste is when you go through the motions of getting to know someone but never get beneath the surface. If you're going to stay on a superficial level with the people with whom you spend your time, you may as well stay home and watch TV.

ᗡᏍ ᗡᏍ ᗡᏍ

"ICE-BREAKING" QUESTIONS

1. What are you most passionate about?
   • Where did this interest come from?
2. What kind of work do you do?
   • What do you love about it?
   • What about it challenges you the most?
   • What about it frustrates you the most?
   • What is your dream regarding your work?
3. What have been the major accomplishments of your life so far?
   • What do you consider your biggest failures?
4. What's the best thing that's happened to you in the last year?
   • What's the worst thing?
5. What would you do if you didn't have to work?
6. Describe your ideal vacation.
7. Would you like to be famous?
   • If yes, what would you like to be famous for?

- If not, why not?
- (If he is famous) What do you like/dislike about being famous?

8. If you were given $ 20 million tomorrow, what would you do with it?
9. What was it like growing up in your family?
   - What good qualities do you attribute to your upbringing?
   - What qualities do you fear you have as a result of your upbringing?
10. Describe what kind of relationship you want.
11. Are you romantic?
    - If yes, in what way(s)?
12. How do you think men are different from women?
13. What makes you happy?
14. What makes you sad?
15. What were you like as a child?
16. As a child, what did you want to be when you grew up?
    - As an adult, what do you want to be when you grow up?
17. What do you think makes you different from other people?
18. Do you believe in God?
    - What is your concept of her/him?
19. To what extent do you feel your actions as an individual can affect social change?
20. What do you consider the three most important social issues today?
    - What would you do about them if you could?

You can add any questions you'd like to this list. What do you really want to know about someone? Just ask.

Watch out that you don't interview men as a way of "getting something". There's a difference between being interested in someone as a fellow human being and interviewing him for the job of "prospective husband."

And there's no reason to confine intimacy to the men you date. Why not connect on a deeper level with friends and people with whom you work?

Many women who have taken "Connecting" reported that, at first, they felt awkward about getting intimate with people and they doubted they could pull it off. If you feel this way, don't let it stop you from plunging ahead. As usual, taking action is the best way to dispel the awkwardness.

Even those women who experienced initial trepidation found they were able to master the art of intimacy with a little practice.

BEING A HOST

A good way to develop the talent of becoming intimate with men is to practice being the "host" instead of a guest in your relationships. Consider the difference between a guest at a party and its host: a guest is there to find out if it's a good party and to be entertained if it is. A host is there to make sure it's a good party and to see to it that the guests are enjoying themselves. To the extent that you're waiting for a man to initiate intimacy and carry the relationship, you're playing the role of guest rather than host.

Being the host in a relationship does not mean you're always the one who plans what you do on dates. It does mean that you see to it that he has a good time rather than waiting for him to provide a good time for you.

Most single people play the role of guest in their relationships, and this is their loss. There's great satisfaction in being the host, in generating the fun, intimacy and excitement. When you consider it your job to make sure *he* has a great time on a date with you, *you'll* end up having a better time. In an ideal relationship, each partner is a host and neither relies on the other to provide the energy and enthusiasm or to "make it happen."

When you assume the role of host in your relationships, you become the kind of person about whom people say, "I have fun and feel good about myself when I'm around her."

ꜱꜱ ꜱꜱ ꜱꜱ

ASSIGNMENT #11:
GET INTIMATE WITH A MAN.

You can use the "20 questions" provided, prepare your own, or wing it. The important thing is to make sure you don't stay safe and superficial. Take risks. And *listen* to his answers.

I will get intimate with _____

by_____
           date

ASSIGNMENT #12:
PLAN A PARTY.

The purpose of this assignment is for you to practice being a host. At your party, you should have your attention on your guests and on making sure they're having a good time. The party doesn't have to be a huge bash; it could be three friends for lunch. Preferably, it should include men.

MY PARTY WILL BE HELD ON _____ AT _____.
                                      date   time
I WILL INVITE:

Notes On This Chapter:

13

Wave Your Magic Wand

YOU HAVE A TOOL FOR MAKING YOUR RELATIONSHIPS MIRACULOUS.

Most of the stories about men and women that our parents read to us when we were children ended when the couple got together. We were told, "They lived happily ever after," but we never got any details about how. The story of Cinderella was no exception — that is, until now. An archaeologist friend of mine recently discovered the original manuscript of the tale in a remote European village, buried under the ruins of what she believes was the prince's castle.

My friend gave me permission to reveal the content to you. Here, at last, is the story of what happened after the wedding:

CINDERELLA: THE SEQUEL

Cinderella and the prince were blissfully happy for the

first few months. He treated her like a queen. He complimented her 10 times a day and made passionate love to her at night. He even sought her advice about how to run the kingdom. He brought her a pair of shoes from every village in his kingdom until her collection filled 28 closets.

There was only one small problem. The prince was not a particularly introspective guy, and he rarely, if ever, talked about how he felt. (It's not clear from the manuscript whether he even knew how he felt most of the time). Cinderella saw this trait as "insensitivity." She complained to the prince that he was not in touch with his feelings, to which he just shrugged.

Cinderella was determined to fix this flaw in the prince's otherwise impeccable character. She kept trying to get him to stop being so withdrawn and uncommunicative.

He did make an effort to express his feelings on a few occasions, but he was quite inept at it. Cinderella tried to explain what he was doing wrong: "That's not letting me know how you're really feeling, it's just throwing a temper trantrum," she would say. Or, "You're not confiding in me, you're just feeling sorry for yourself."

When Cinderella's friends would tell her, "You're so lucky to be married to the Prince," she would say, "That's what you think. It may look like a good marriage but he never opens up to me. You don't know how awful it is to feel like you're living with a stranger."

Cinderella kept working on the problem. She pointed out to the prince that he bought her shoes as a substitute for expressing his affection. After that, he stopped buying her shoes. She complained that there was something missing from their lovemaking because she didn't know what he was really thinking. He began making love to her less frequently.

Pretty soon, the prince stopped consulting Cinderella about matters of state and stopped giving her compliments. In fact, he stopped talking to her very much at all, and he began scheduling longer and more frequent trips away from the castle.

It was at this point in the story that the manuscript left off. The remaining text had apparently been chewed up by rats. The barely legible words just before the bite marks were, "their differences were irreconcilable . . ."

This ending shouldn't really come as much of a surprise. After all, it's more or less what has happened to many of the relationships you've observed, isn't it?

But things didn't have to turn out that way. Cinderella didn't realize it, but she had a "magic wand," a powerful tool with which she could have prevented her relationship from falling apart. It may be too late for Cinderella to live happily ever after with her prince, but it's not too late for you.

A POWER TOOL

The magic wand that can help you prevent unhappy endings is called "empowerment." Empower means "to give power to." Other ways to express this idea are "to give energy to; to give attention to; to emphasize." When we empower something, its importance grows. We make a big deal out of it, and therefore it becomes a big deal.

You're already using the tool of empowerment. However, most of the time you're not using it effectively.

Take the way my friend's teenaged daughter deals with pimples. When Candace gets a pimple, she touches it, tries to make it go away, and continually checks to see if it's still there. When someone tells her she looks nice, she says, "I do not. Look at this giant zit on my chin." Candace uses empowerment to make her pimples a much bigger part of her life than they would be if she just ignored them and left them alone. This is an example of an ineffective use of empowerment.

You're always empowering something — whatever you focus your energy and attention on. The problem is that most of us tend to empower the negative things in our lives. For some reason, our attention seems to get drawn to mistakes and imperfections, while we often take for granted or fail to notice the things that are going well. To an extent, this approach is practical — we need to pay some attention to the things that are wrong in our lives and to fix them.

But most people carry this practice way too far. They don't realize that what they're doing when they empower a problem is making it bigger. What this does to relationships can be best illustrated with a simple set of diagrams.

Let's call circle #1 your relationship. You just met him and you're doing great together. He has no visible faults. You love the way he picks up his coffee cup, the way he dresses, the way he smiles at you. The happy looking flowers inside the circle stand for all the good things: you have fun, you share an interest in astronomy, he takes you to great places, you really like his friends, etc. You "water" the flowers by paying attention to and appreciating these qualities (as indicated by the arrows).

CIRCLE #1

In circle #2, about six months have gone by and now a problem has come up in the relationship: You want him to call you whenever he's going to be late, but he never does. The arrows are the attention you pay to this problem by complaining about his inconsiderate behavior to him and to your friends, and by getting into fights with him over it. With so much energy being diverted to this problem, there's not much left over for the good things, and the flowers are beginning to wilt.

CIRCLE #2

In circle #3, it's a few months later and almost all your attention is going to this problem. It has escalated out of proportion. You now see his inconsiderateness as a major character flaw. You think he's selfish and doesn't care about you. What's more, you've got lots of evidence to prove it. The relationship isn't working and you're ready to say goodbye.

The flowers, meanwhile, are dying because they aren't being watered. You're not having fun together any more. You may still go to great places but you don't appreciate them because all you do when you're there is argue.

You empowered what began as a minor irritation until it has become all there is to the relationship.

CIRCLE #3

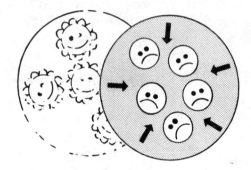

YOU LIVE WITH WHAT YOU EMPOWER

There are degrees of empowerment. In the preceeding example, the problem was empowered so much that it destroyed the relationship, choking the spirit out of it entirely.

But sometimes you only empower a problem enough to make it a constant "issue" or source of irritation (as in, "You never pick up your towels" or "I hate it that you keep falling asleep in front of the TV"). In these cases, you don't destroy the relationship, you just make it less fun. It's like having a low-grade infection — you're not really sick but you're not really well either.

We all know couples who have been together for years and are still griping about the same things. My girlfriend's parents are a classic example. For 40 years, she's been nagging at him about the fact that he forgets birthdays, and he's been getting mad at her for spending too much money on clothes. They'll never get divorced over these issues, but as long as they keep empowering them, they'll keep being upset with each other.

Complaining about a problem is like scratching a sore — it makes it worse *and* it makes it hang around longer. But because they love to complain, most people never seem to notice that it's counterproductive. It doesn't solve problems, and it isn't a very effective way of adapting to them.

ANATOMY OF A RELATIONSHIP

At this point in "Connecting," I do an experiment with the participants. I ask a few of them to describe the best relationship they ever had and what made it so great. They start out talking about the good things: "We talked a lot and cuddled a lot and he was very romantic." They usually cover that part in about 30 seconds.

Then they get to the part about what went wrong: " . . . but then I started to have to work a lot and he didn't like that, and then he started spending a lot of time with a close female friend and I got jealous, and then . . . "

I usually have to cut them off about two minutes into the "what went wrong" part. I point out that I never even asked them to describe what went wrong. They start to see that what they did in the excercise is just like what they did in the relationship. They slipped into focusing their attention on whatever wasn't going well, and stopped appreciating the things that were great.

At this point, they usually say, "Aha, no wonder the relationship ended. We started taking the good things for granted and paying too much attention to the bad things, until the good things disappeared."

Just as something you give attention to gets stronger, something that's not appreciated will diminish. When you stop noticing and appreciating someone's good qualities, you lose sight of what it was that made you fall in love with them.

Knowing this, I'm very careful to thank Tony for things that I might be tempted to take for granted. I thank him every time we go out for dinner. When we have a good talk, I thank him for confiding in me and for being such a great friend. I try not to let any of the things I appreciate about him or our relationship go unacknowledged.

CONFESSIONS OF A FORMER CRITIC

The principles of empowerment apply to other areas of your life besides relationships. I first learned about this principle when I worked for a corporation that conducted time management seminars. After becoming a successful seminar leader, I was promoted to training new leaders. I knew what qualities were and weren't effective in leading seminars, but what I didn't know was how to help the trainees bring out the good qualities in themselves and get rid of the bad ones.

When I first started this job, I would put the trainees in front of the group one at a time and have them practice leading a seminar for about 15 or 20 minutes. I'd write little notes about things they said and did, and afterward I'd tell them what corrections to make. I'd give them constructive criticism such as, "You didn't speak loudly enough, you didn't make that point very clearly, and you never answered Arnie's question."

After about three or four hours of working this way, people could barely open their mouths in front of the group. Clearly, something wasn't working. It was obvious to me that I had an unusually inept group of trainees.

I asked Frank, an experienced trainer of seminar leaders, to sit in on one of my sessions so he could see how slow these people were. He saw right away what the real problem was. He explained that because I was focusing on the trainees' flaws and inadequacies, those were getting more pronounced. He said, "People are always going to make mistakes; if you keep working on their imperfections they're not going to improve."

The approach I had been using to train seminar leaders was a variation of the same approach I had used to turn powerful men into weak ones (the sabotage pattern I told you about in Chapter 8, remember?). In both cases, I was very perceptive about what people were doing wrong and very accurate in the corrections I made and the advice I gave them. But I was ineffective both with men and with the seminar leaders because under my influence, they got worse instead of better.

In both cases, the turning point came when I saw that the approach I had inadvertantly been using to tear people down could be used to build them up. Seeing the principle in operation was what enabled me to turn it around.

Frank's advice was to use the same techniques I had been using on the seminar leader trainees, but in reverse. "If you work on their strengths, they'll begin to blossom," he told me. "You'll never make them perfect, but when you emphasize their strong points, they'll start to naturally overcome many of their weaknesses."

I started out my next training session the same way I had before. I put the trainees in front of the room and wrote little notes about their performances. But this time I told them all the things they did right. I said things like, "It was great the way you got Joe's attention, you really knew the material, and your joke really broke the ice." The difference was remarkable. They started to improve right away. (This really is magic!)

Empowering their strengths didn't mean I stopped pointing out what they were doing wrong. After they achieved a degree of confidence, I might throw in something like, "Next time, speak a little louder." But whereas before when I had told them they weren't speaking loudly enough they didn't improve, now they did start speaking more loudly.

I let them know that I was their fan, that I appreciated how good they were, that I wanted them to make it, and that I knew they could. They began to want to make corrections for me. They started blossoming around me instead of wilting like they had when I had focused on what was wrong with them.

It's even easier to see this principle from the other side. You don't shine around people who keep pointing out your flaws and inadequacies. When you think of the times you gained a skill or did particularly well at something, it was probably when someone was empowering your strengths.

I like the way Ralph Waldo Emerson expressed the idea of empowerment. He said "Omit the negative proposition and chant only the beauty of the good."

WHAT TO DO ABOUT FLAWS

Does this mean I think you should adopt a Pollyanna attitude and ignore problems? No. What I'm saying is that you shouldn't handle problems in ways that make them get worse instead of better.

It doesn't hurt to try to change something you don't like about your mate, as long as you don't make a career out of it. As we've already established, complaining about the problem never works. Sometimes making a request about it does work.

Once when we were first married, I got sick and had to stay in bed. It was then that I discovered that Tony was insensitive about sickness. This was a major flaw with which I started to do battle immediately. (This was before I knew how to use empowerment.)

At first I tried to make him see how insensitive he was. "How can you come in here and ask me if I want to go to a movie?," I exclaimed dramatically. "Can't you see I'm sick?" An hour later he came in and asked me if I could proofread a report he was preparing. I said, "You're so insensitive, how can you ask me to do something like that when I'm sick?" This kind of friction continued for two or three days.

I shared my exasperation with a friend. Her advice was, "Tell him what you want from him instead of what you don't want." At first I argued, "I shouldn't have to tell him how to treat a sick person," but finally, I decided to try it. When he came home that night I said, "I would really like it if you would bring me some soup." He was more than happy to comply. Then I said, "Would you please read to me and stroke my head? He said, "Sure."

I was thrilled to find that a simple request was all that had stood between friction and harmony. But I soon discovered there were other problems that could not be resolved this way. After my success in getting Tony to change his behavior when I was sick, I tried to apply the request technique to a Really Big Challenge:

Tony is good about cleaning up and he washes the dishes more readily than I do, but one thing he never does is throw away an empty can. I can remember walking into the kitchen each night and getting upset over the empty soft drink or beer can on the counter, the one blight in an otherwise spotless kitchen.

You can't imagine what I went through trying to get him to throw away empty cans, I tried complaining, nagging, threatening, cajoling, bribing, and analyzing. Nothing worked. I empowered this problem to the point where you would think we were talking about dead bodies on the counter.

Then I tried making a simple request. This worked no better. So much for my new "secret weapon."

Finally, I weighed Tony's inability to throw away cans against his good features. When I stacked up "good father, kind, fun, sexy, good provider, and best friend" against "leaves cans on the counter," I finally got my sense of humor back. Once I started to laugh at this problem I began to actually find Tony's habit endearing.

There is still an empty can on my kitchen counter almost every night, but they don't bother me anymore. In fact, these cans have become a source of entertainment for our family and friends.

ON ACCEPTANCE

How do you think you would react if someone you loved had only one arm? You would probably accept it. People are good at accepting things that they know they can't change. It's the flaws you think you *can* change that drive you crazy.

Everyone, including you, has flaws. The perfect person does not exist. Try accepting your partner's flaws and being grateful for all the wonderful qualities that outweigh them, instead of trying to get rid of all his faults.

Maybe you can train children to stop doing things you don't like, but with most adults, it's a losing battle. Let's face it, if he's made it this far with a bad habit intact, he's probably not going to give it up now. If he's a person who always loses his keys, he's probably not going to start keeping track of them just because it drives you crazy. If he's been ten minutes late for everything for the past 30 years, he's not going to become punctual just because you don't like waiting for him.

But while he was collecting all those annoying habits he was also developing the character and richer sense of identity that come with age. Along with his flaws, he comes equipped with increased sensitivity, understanding, and insight of a mature adult.

After you've lived on your own and become "set in your ways," it may be harder for you to adjust to someone else's habits. Having an "untrained" person in your environment is bound to cause some irritation. He's sure to leave too much of a mess or put the silverware away in the wrong drawer. But these minor irritations of cohabitation are a small price to pay for the excitement, passion, and pleasure of a loving relationship.

EMPOWERMENT NOW

You don't have to wait until you live with someone to start putting empowerment to work in your relationships. You can start empowering the next man you meet by looking for his strengths instead of his shortcomings.

When you tell your friends you are dating a new man who is "nice, but doesn't have good posture" or "attractive, but a bit overweight" you are empowering the negative. Not only are you emphasizing those features to yourself, but you're setting up a negative expectation on the part of your friends. When they meet this man, they are going to be focusing on his posture and weight because that's what you've made them aware of.

Empowerment is as valuable in work situations as it is in relationships. The experience I had in training seminar leaders is only one example. I'll bet if you look you'll find dozens of little ways in which you are empowering the negative aspects of your job and the people with whom you work.

You'll be amazed at the results you'll get when you start to reverse this practice. Start becoming the kind of person that brings out the best in people, and you'll find yourself working (and playing) with the best people.

Last but not least, you can get incredible results by using empowerment on *yourself.* The next chapter tells you how to do this.

ᗞ ᗞ ᗞ

ASSIGNMENT #13: COMPLIMENT ONE MAN EACH DAY.

You can compliment men you are dating or men with whom you work, whether or not they are "available." Be sure your compliments are personal, not, "That was a good report you turned in" or "That sandwich looks delicious."

The compliments can be about his physical appearance: "That's a beautiful sweater; you always dress so nicely" or about his personality, "You're always so attentive when people speak to you; you're really a good listener."

Although they might be embarrassed by them, people love hearing compliments. A compliment can make someone's day.

Doing this assignment will help you get used to empowering people, pointing to and bringing out their good qualities. You can't overdo this — if you feel like it, give compliments to 20 men a day. Give compliments to women, too. Don't be surprised if people start flocking to you because they feel so appreciated by you.

Notes On This Chapter:

14

Claim Your Crown

TRANSFORM YOURSELF INTO THE WOMAN
YOU'VE ALWAYS WANTED TO BE.

Do you know that you're a great catch? Do you think any
man would be extremely lucky to end up with you? Do you
consider yourself a prize? A "10?" A dream come true?

If you don't, you're in good company. Unfortunately,
most people suffer from low self-esteem. Even those who
give themselves high marks in most areas of their lives
usually have a few areas in which they consider themselves
losers.

In an earlier chapter I mentioned the Groucho Marx joke:
"I would never want to belong to any club that would have
someone like me as a member." It's no joke that many
women hold themselves in such low esteem that they think
there must be something wrong with any man who would
want them as a mate. When I first began living with Tony, I
discovered that this attitude can be contagious.

Tony had come home from an evening "out with the guys." He told me about an attractive woman who had tried to pick him up at the bar where he and his friends had gotten together.

He was not talking about this woman to make me jealous; he was just telling me about his evening. It was clear that he had no interest in her. But instead of making me feel good — after all, he had come home to me — hearing about this woman made me start to feel insecure about myself.

"Was she really pretty?" I asked him. "She was thinner than I am, wasn't she?" "What was she like?" "I'll bet your friends thought you were a fool not to get her number."

As I expressed these insecurities, I noticed Tony's attitude start to subtly change. My doubts about myself seemed to be rubbing off on him. It was as though my lack of respect for his choice of me made him question this choice.

I guess my confidence in myself and my certainty that I was the right woman for Tony were stronger than my insecurities, because suddenly, something clicked, and I saw there was nothing to be insecure about.

I said in a carefree way, "Well, of course, she might be thinner than I am, but no one is better for you than me." He seemed to brighten. Whereas my doubts about myself had made him start to feel unsure, my confidence in myself made him feel good about being with me.

Everybody knows "you've got to value and love yourself first if you want someone else to love you." But knowing this doesn't seem to make a difference.

You can readily see that the attitude, "Any man who would love me is smart" is better than, "I'm not worthy of love." But knowing this doesn't necessarily help you change your feelings about yourself.

What you need is a practical way to raise your self-esteem. You need a tool.

ALL-PURPOSE TOOL

The tool for raising your self-esteem is the same tool you learned about in the last chapter: empowerment. Like charity, empowerment begins at home. In the case of your self image, it has already begun.

One of the reasons why you don't value yourself enough is that you've been using the tool of empowerment to magnify your faults. You've been paying a lot more attention to your flaws and the things you don't like about yourself than to your strengths and the things about yourself you do value.

You look for your faults, work on them, emphasize them, and reinforce them. You're much quicker to point them out when they show up than you are to pat yourself on the back when you exhibit one of your strengths.

You slant the truth, saying things like, "I'm always late" whenever you don't arrive at an appointment on time. You're not *always* late — the truth is sometimes you're late and sometimes you're on time. You're probably on time more often than you're late, but when you get somewhere on time you don't say, "I'm always on time."

You constantly make negative pronouncements about yourself: "I have no discipline; I'm too indecisive; I'm overweight;" etc. When you make a mistake you say, "I'm so dumb; I have the worst memory; I always put my foot in my mouth."

Even when you do acknowledge a strength, you're quick to point out that it isn't good enough. "I always remember birthdays — but I can never make up my mind about which card to send." "I'm a good cook — but that's not going to help me get rich." "This shade of blue looks good on me — but I look too fat in this dress." "So what that I'm a great organizer — that isn't what men are looking for in a woman."

If you had a friend that was as critical of you as you are of yourself, you would have broken off the friendship long ago. You wouldn't want to be around someone who constantly pointed out your shortcomings, yet that's what you do to yourself.

Okay, you're not perfect. But must you keep dwelling on your imperfections? Instead of empowering your faults by constantly focusing attention on them, why not empower your strengths?

This *is* as simple as it sounds, but that doesn't mean it is easy. The techniques in this chapter will work, but only if you apply them. A lifelong habit is not often broken overnight. You're going to need to monitor your thoughts to make sure that your habit of empowering the negative doesn't creep back in when you're not looking. It's going to take discipline and work, but the results will be well worth it. Doing this will turn your life around.

ফ্স ফ্স ফ্স

EXERCISE: ASSET INVENTORY (part one)

On the list on the next page, check off every personality trait that applies to you. It's okay to check as many traits as you like.

ASSET INVENTORY

___thoughtful
___perceptive
___humorous
___lively
___active
___trusting
___outgoing
___funny
___accurate
___gracious
___energetic
___consistent
___witty
___ambitious
___intuitive
___articulate
___quiet
___helpful
___industrious
___fearless
___decisive
___bold
___intense
___determined
___clever
___rational
___brave
___relaxed
___sociable
___competent
___expressive
___secure
___sincere
___influential
___fair
___charming
___cheerful
___tactful
___pretty
___spontaneous
___fit
___stylish
___savvy
___talented
___empathetic

___visionary
___thorough
___mature
___original
___flexible
___cooperative
___organized
___game
___curious
___patient
___prompt
___powerful
___healthy
___competitive
___attractive
___daring
___adventurous
___affectionate
___responsible
___respectful
___vigorous
___dependable
___protective
___resourceful
___persuasive
___capable
___diplomatic
___candid
___safe
___upbeat
___even-tempered
___easy-going
___casual
___enthusiastic
___generous
___liberal
___loyal
___calm
___fun
___entrepreneurial
___enterprising
___brilliant
___compassionate
___good listener
___insightful

___straightforward
___sweet
___tolerant
___forthright
___open
___courageous
___assertive
___creative
___friendly
___wise
___amusing
___peaceful
___modest
___humane
___humble
___honest
___original
___visual
___appreciative
___responsive
___dependable
___inspiring
___smart
___persistent
___bright
___diligent
___sophisticated
___direct
___caring
___sensitive
___sharp
___intellectual
___tender
___kind
___steady
___stirring
___tasteful
___conscientious
___warm
___dynamic
___athletic
___cuddly
___well-read
___
___

EXERCISE: ASSET INVENTORY (part two)

Pick two traits you checked that you particularly like about yourself. Use the space below to list 10 pieces of evidence "proving" that you have those traits. The evidence doesn't have to be dramatic and significant: it can be a small gesture you made, a little thing you did that no one even noticed, or something someone said. But it should all be current. Stick to things that happened during the last month.

For example, evidence that you're "fun" might be the surprise lunch you threw for a co-worker who was retiring; a friend telling you he enjoyed the evening you spent together last week; or the time everyone was gathered around your desk at work, telling jokes.

Evidence that you're "spontaneous" might be that you called a friend to go to a movie on the spur of the moment, or that you stopped off to take a walk along the beach on your way home from work.

Evidence that you're "generous" could be that you offered to stay late at work or that you picked up the check at dinner.

Ten pieces of evidence that I'm _____ are:

quality #1

1.

2.

3.

4.

5.

6.

7.

8.

9.

10.

Ten pieces of evidence that I'm _____are:

quality #2

1.

2.

3.

4.

5.

6.

7.

8.

9.

10.

How easy was it to come up with 10 pieces of evidence for your strengths? Pretty difficult, huh? Don't worry — this was just a warm-up exercise to start getting you in the habit of empowering your good qualities. You're not expected to be an expert yet.

How much easier do you think it would have been if I had asked you to list 10 pieces of evidence for two of your flaws? A lot easier, right? You're so used to empowering your faults that the examples would probably roll right off your pen. You could confine the evidence to the last three days and it would still be easy. (If you're tempted to try it in order to find out just how easy it is, don't. That's a habit you're trying to kick, remember?).

You can start right away (and continue for the rest of your life) to use the tool of empowerment to bring out your strengths. When you catch yourself empowering a flaw, stop. Instead, remind yourself of something you did well or something you like about yourself. Remember, whatever you empower is what you live with, so empower those things you want to see more of.

TAKING A STAND

One of the ways to do this is by "taking a stand" about yourself. To take a stand, you first identify two or three qualities that you would like to bring out in yourself.

The words you choose to describe the qualities of your "stand" are most important. They most be bold and power-ful — extraordinary rather than ordinary, exaggerated rather than understated. Whereas your normal tendency is to be modest in describing your positive attributes, in tak-ing a stand you should be anything but.

Under normal circumstances you might describe your-self as "attractive." But if you wanted to include a statement about your appearance in your stand, you would never choose a word as wimpy as that. You would use "gorgeous," or "stunning," or "exquisite" or "beautiful." Get the drift?

It may feel uncomfortable to describe yourself in such glowing terms. It may seem that you are being conceited or that you are bragging. If it does, you're on the right track!

Your stand doesn't have to be realistic and the qualities don't have to be ones you already see in yourself. In fact, your stand should be "a stretch" — it should seem almost out of reach.

A stand is something "made up," — not the objective truth. What makes it true is your commitment to it and empowerment of it. Your stand should not be based on what you think you could or couldn't be, it should be based on what you want to be and what you're committed to being. After all, if you're making something up, you may as well make it up the way you want it.

You're already making up stands about yourself. Maybe you think, "I could never take the stand that I'm gorgeous because I'm not that attractive." But it's because you've (unwittingly) taken a stand that you're *not* attractive that you describe yourself that way.

Those negative things you say about yourself: "I'm not that attractive; I always forget names; I don't stick up for myself enough; I'm lazy," all are stands you've taken about yourself and empowered.

Whatever stand you take and empower is what you make more real in your life. My stand is, "I'm glamorous and dynamic, and people blossom around me." Believe me, if you could see me when I wake up most mornings, it's the last thing you would say about me. But by taking this stand and working with it (we'll get to how you work with your stand soon), I have actually been able to bring out those qualities in myself more and more.

Obviously, taking a stand that you have red hair if you're a brunette will not make your hair red. But there are very few qualities that are objectively one way or another. You have much more power to affect how you see yourself (and thus how other people see you) than you think.

You've been using this power all along. But you've been using it "by accident." Now, by consciously taking a stand, you're going to use that power "on purpose."

STANDING BEHIND YOUR STAND

When John F. Kennedy said in the beginning of his presidency that we would have a man on the moon within the decade, he was taking a stand. He had no evidence that we would reach this lofty goal; in fact, at the time it didn't seem possible that it could be accomplished. Without JFK's "stand," without his commitment to this achievement, that "giant leap for mankind" might not have occurred until many years later.

There are all kinds of stands. A company takes a stand when it claims, "We offer the best service in the industry," or "No one can beat our prices," or "We make the world's greatest hamburgers."

Taking a stand is meaningless unless you stand behind it. Unless you empower it, it will not have much of an impact on your life.

There are several ways to empower your stand:

1. COLLECT EVIDENCE

In part two of the "ASSET INVENTORY" exercise earlier in this chapter, you practiced collecting evidence. The evidence you collect for your stand, like the evidence you wrote down in that exercise, can consist of small words and gestures. If your stand is, "I'm gorgeous," don't wait for someone to come up to you and say, "You're the most gorgeous woman I've ever seen," as your evidence. Someone saying, "That's a pretty dress" or "I like your hair" is fine.

You should get into the habit of looking at everything you possibly can as evidence for your stand, and get out of the habit of invalidating the evidence that tells you that you're terrific: "He told me I have beautiful eyes, but so what, he's married; Four guys approached me at the party but they were all nerds; He told me he had a wonderful time last night but he didn't sound sincere."

Remember the analogy we used earlier in the book — the one about the lawyer who could argue either side of a case.

A good lawyer would never ignore a piece of evidence that supported her case, no matter how small. And she would never include evidence of the opposing view in building her case. Always argue *for* your stand and consider anything that contradicts it inadmissible evidence.

2. USE YOUR STAND AS A "ROLE MODEL"

Chris' stand was, "I am exciting, compassionate, and gracious." In "Connecting," she asked me for advice about how to talk to her boyfriend about a delicate problem that had arisen. I asked her, "What would someone who is 'exciting, compassionate, and gracious' say?" She paused for a moment, then her face lit up. She had her answer.

You can use your stand as though it is your own personal "board of directors" and turn to it for guidance, advice, and inspiration. The more you base your actions and decisions on your stand, the more you will become it.

If there is a person who epitomizes the qualities of your stand, you can use that person as a role model. You can ask yourself "What would Grace Kelly have done in this situation? What would Diane Sawyer do?"

3. LOOK THE PART

In an earlier chapter we talked about the importance of appearance. Now, you can use your stand to enhance your attractiveness. When you are shopping you can apply the "role model" technique and ask yourself, "Does that look like something a woman who is 'glamorous, provocative, and tender' would wear?" to help you make decisions about what to buy.

When you go shopping, be open to taking risks with your presentation instead of choosing the kind of clothes you always wear. Try on clothes that you may think you can't afford or that you would "never buy." Don't be afraid to enlist the help of salespeople. They are often experts at helping you achieve a particular look. And browze through fashion magazines with your stand in mind.

In "Connecting," I have clothing, hair, and make-up professionals come in for one session to help the participants bring out their stands in their looks. Getting your hair styled or your make-up done with the qualities of your stand in mind will help you express them in your appearance.

When Judy began "Connecting," she was a walking advertisement for the refugee look. Disheveled and definitely *not* glamorous, she always wore dresses that resembled sacks. I had never heard anyone choose a stand that was more of "a stretch" than her's. It was, "I am glamorous, sexy, and striking."

I encouraged her to buy some new clothes, to have her hair and make-up styled, and to get contact lenses or a more attractive pair of glasses. When she came back the following week, several people in the course did not recognize her! She had followed through on my suggestions and had literally transformed herself — she *was* glamorous, sexy, and striking. She was an inspiration to everyone in the course.

Later, she called to tell me that after having had only six dates over the previous four months, three men had asked her out during the last week. It wasn't only because of the difference in her looks — it was because she felt differently about herself.

4. ADVERTISE

Post signs around your house with your stand written on them. Place them in strategic places like the inside of your closet door, on your bathroom mirror, and on your refrigerator door. You can also put them on the dashboard of your car and on your desk at work. They will remind you of the qualities you are empowering and help you keep them in your thoughts.

⤞ ⤞ ⤞

EXERCISE: TAKE A STAND

The following list of words is based on stands taken by women in "Connecting" courses. Of course, there are many qualities that are not represented on this list, but it will provide you with some good ideas.

Choose a stand that expresses the way you would like to be. Make sure you "go for it" — don't use any bland, run-of-the-mill words. "Okay," "nice," and "cute" do not belong in your stand.

Don't make your stand too long. Any more than about three qualities or phrases will tend to diminish its impact.

Select a stand that will make you feel good about yourself vis à vis your relationships with men. "I'm competent, organized, and motivated" may be a great stand to take when you're job-hunting but there are probably better qualities to emphasize when you're man-hunting.

To help you select the right words for your stand, ask yourself, "How would I love to hear a man describe me?"

SAMPLE ADJECTIVES FOR STANDS

Exquisite	Sensual	Delicate
Glamorous	Sexy	Tender
Gorgeous	Outrageous	Soft
Chic	Sophisticated	Feminine
Elegant	Smart	Vivacious
Stunning	Stellar	Exuberant
Voluptuous	Creative	Adventurous
Exotic	Extraordinary	Worldly
Extraordinary	Magnanimous	Cultured
Seductive	Inviting	Stimulating
Sultry	Intelligent	Powerful
Enticing	Magnificent	Generous
Scintillating	Inspiring	Fun-loving
Expressive	Strong	Adventurous
Beautiful	Fun	Fascinating
Unpredictable	Funny	Powerful
Irresistible	Charming	Brilliant
Generous	Gracious	Bold
Exciting	Wealthy	Exquisite
Dynamic	Warm	Inspiring
Adorable	Affectionate	Loving
Cuddly	Original	Lovable
Striking	Fantastic	Elegant

SAMPLE PHRASES FOR STANDS

People blossom around me.
I am the stuff dreams are made of.
Men are drawn to me.
I am a "10."
I am one of a kind.
I'm what every man wants.

My stand is: _____

⮑ ⮑ ⮑

ASSIGNMENT #14:
COLLECT ONE PIECE OF EVIDENCE
EACH DAY FOR YOUR STAND.

Remember, evidence comes in all sizes. To help you get into the habit of finding evidence for your stand, you may want to keep up this exercise for longer than a week.

ASSIGNMENT #15:
"PURGE" YOUR CLOSET.

If you're like most people, you're happy with only about half the clothes in your closet. The remaining items are "things that might come back into style," "bargains," and the 43 old shirts you're keeping to wear when you paint.

Each time you bought a pair of pants, a blouse, or a skirt on sale, you probably said, "For $30.00 I can't go wrong." But guess what — you've gone wrong 20 times for $30.00.

Mix-and-match ensembles that all look like the same outfit do not help you express your stand. Neither do clothes that are cheap, unflattering, or in need of repair. Wearing clothes in which you do not feel attractive diminishes your self-esteem.

It's time to clear out everything in your closet that does not help you look and feel your best. Doing this will help you make room for new clothes that do represent your stand.

Invite your support partner to come over and help you purge your closet. Tell her/him to be especially tough in encouraging you to part with clothes that don't make you look your best.

ASSIGNMENT #16:
DO ONE THING TO HAVE
YOUR APPEARANCE REFLECT YOUR STAND.

After you purge your closet, you'll probably want to buy a new article of clothing, a belt, or a pair of shoes. Or, you can do something new with your hair or make-up, or get a manicure or a pedicure. Do anything you'd like to help you bring out your stand in your appearance.

Notes On This Chapter:

15

Lead A Charmed Life

IF YOU COULD HAVE THE KIND OF RELATIONSHIP
YOU REALLY WANTED, WHAT WOULD IT BE LIKE?

As we've already established, the days when mating
was necessary for survival are ancient history. The days
when it was motivated by purely functional concerns are
recent history. Some futurists predict that in the absence of
these compelling motivations, mating itself will become a
thing of the past. Others say our strong needs for intimacy
and companionship will always provide motivation for men
and women to join together.

Whatever future course civilization takes, one thing is
certain. As an individual looking forward to the prospect of
getting married in today's world — you stand at an important crossroads.

Behind you are the many unsuccessful relationships
you've observed and experienced. In earlier chapters of this
book you swept away much of the debris — the negative

attitudes and patterns — they left in their wake. These relationships were instructive as well as destructive, leaving you with a clear picture of what you *don't* want. What they didn't leave you with was a clear picture of what you *do* want.

You probably have a good idea of what kind of relationship you'd be "willing to settle for." You probably know what kind is "as good as it gets," "the best you can do," or "better than nothing." You're smart enough to know that a relationship "won't be easy," "won't solve all your problems," and will require "sacrifice and compromise."

There's nothing wrong with being practical and having realistic goals and expectations. But you have a problem when you confuse "what you want" with "what you think you can get." That problem is compounded by the fact that what may have once been "realistic" expectations about relationships, no longer are.

New social conditions, new men, and new women add up to a new ballgame. The rules for this game have not yet been written. You get to write them, at least for yourself. The limitations and restrictions of the past are not the guidelines you should use to create the relationship of the present.

You're all too familiar with relationships the old way: Compromise and sacrifice. Adversarial politics. Win/lose or lose/lose. Emotions overly controlled or out-of-control. Putting up with it for sake of the children. Complaining, nagging, fighting, bickering. Trapped. Cheating. Pain. Even the good ones seem to have their share of conflicting goals, hurt feelings, and friction.

But have you ever stopped to imagine what a great relationship might be like? Not the "Ozzie and Harriet" and "Father Knows Best" variety between smiling cardboard cut-outs whose only resemblance to real people is that they need to mow the lawn once a week.

What about the ingredients that might be present in a truly fantastic relationship between two equal partners:

Harmony. Love. Affection. Win/win. Sharing. Working it out together. There for each other when you need each other. Helping. Patience with each other's faults. Supportive. Best friends. Counseling each other. Passion and romance. Fresh and unpredictable instead of static. Growing closer through conflicts and challenges instead of farther apart. Fun. Adventures. Freedom to go your separate ways when you want to. Privacy when you need it. Happiness. Inspiration.

It's time to put cynicism, skepticism, and realistic expectations aside and to start discovering your vision about relationships. Let's start with a warm-up exercise.

EXERCISE: "WHAT HAS WORKED"

What has worked in your past or present relationships? What are the qualities that made them successful? (Think about your most satisfying relationship):

1.

2.

3.

4.

5.

6.

7.

8.

9.

10.

Many of these same qualities will help you make your future relationships successful.

᪣ ᪣ ᪣

VISUALIZATION:
CREATING IT THE WAY YOU WANT IT

"Visualization" is a technique many professional athletes use to get into the winning spirit and to heighten their abilities. It is nothing more than "imagining" or "daydreaming" about a goal you want to achieve. Many people believe that by getting a clear and tangible mental picture of something they want, they are facilitated in manifesting it.

You can use the technique of visualization to "create" your ideal relationship. The way you do this is to picture what it would be like to be with your husband in a number of different situations.

There are some guidelines that can help you get the most from the process of visualization. Instead of picturing external things — what he looks like, what he does for a living, etc. — you should picture what it feels like to be together.

Don't state things in negative terms: we don't feel trapped; we don't always agree on politics; we don't do everything together. Instead, state things in positive terms: we feel a sense of freedom about being together; we enjoy debating about issues on which we differ; we like to spend time apart as well as together.

Don't overlook the impact of the relationship on *you*.

Many women discover that once they find a relationship, a lot of the energy and drive they put into looking for one is now available to be channeled elsewhere.

That was true for me. After I got married, I found I was able to achieve much more than I had when I was single. This was not only due to the fact that I redirected my energy. It was due in part to the stable foundation with which my marriage provided me. The sense of security I felt in my home life made it easier for me to take risks in my career and my relationships with other people.

⮞⮞ ⮞⮞ ⮞⮞

EXERCISE:
IDEAL RELATIONSHIP VISUALIZATION

Here are some questions to help you get started. Use these as a springboard for visualizing your relationship. Really let your imagination go.

IN MY IDEAL RELATIONSHIP . . .
Qualities of my ideal man:

Things we do together:

What we talk about:

How he treats me:

How I treat him:

What it's like when we're together at home:

What it's like when we're with friends:

What it's like when we're with family:

What it's like when we're at social events:

What our vacations are like:

How we handle our finances:

How we handle disagreements, arguments, fights:

What people say about us as a couple:

How I am different as an individual because of this relationship:

— at work

— with my family

— with friends

— by myself

What else:

In exploring your thoughts and feelings about your ideal relationship, you may have felt some sadness. This is actually a good thing.

Doing this exercise didn't cause the sadness — it merely revealed the pain that was there. Normally, you try to avoid that pain. You lull yourself into a sense of complacency, covering up your strong desire for a relationship with an "I'm okay about being single" attitude.

By doing this exercise, you uncovered some of the frustration and pain you feel about not having a relationship. You can use this pain to strengthen your commitment to finding a relationship and to motivate yourself to take action toward your goal.

🥿 🥿 🥿

ASSIGNMENT #17:
CREATE A RELATIONSHIP "PORTRAIT."

This assignment is a way to take the previous visualization exercise one step further. You'll need poster board, glue, scissors, and a pile of magazines. (It won't hurt to add a box of tissues to the list of supplies — this assignment could be another tear jerker).

First, leaf through the magazines and find pictures that represent your ideal relationship — photographs, images, and words that illustrate your ideas about what you want your relationship to be like. Cut out these pictures and make a collage of them.

People in "Connecting" often react to this assignment by saying, "It sounds silly." But after they do it, the majority of them report that they had a ball with it and that they felt it helped provide them with clearer and more tangible concepts of their ideal relationship.

No two portraits ever look alike. Just use your imagination and creativity, and have fun. You may want to hang your completed portrait somewhere in your home to help you continue visualizing how you want your relationship to be.

When you're finished with your portrait, show it to your partner and explain to her/him what the images represent to you.

ASSIGNMENT #18:
INTERVIEW TWO HAPPILY MARRIED
COUPLES ABOUT THEIR MARRIAGE.

Part one. You can interview them together or separately. Don't be afraid to probe — the couples interviewed by "Connecting" participants have really enjoyed this process and have gotten as much out of it as the interviewers. Ask them about things you really want to know, as well as the following questions:

1. How did they meet?
2. What were their first impressions of each other?
3. When did they realize "this is 'it'?"
4. Did either of them have a fear of commitment?
   a. If so, how did they resolve it?
5. What are the ingredients that have made them a successful couple?
6. How do they handle disagreements?

Part two. After you complete your interviews, have a discussion with your support partner about them. Cover these questions:

1. What did you learn?
2. How can you apply it to your own relationships?
3. What, if anything, did the couples say that surprised you?

Notes On This Chapter:

16

Bring On The Suitors

WITH A WORLD OF RESOURCES AT YOUR FINGERTIPS, FINDING A PRINCE HAS NEVER BEEN SO EASY.

As a single adult woman, you are a member of an elite demographic group, one with the collective buying power to keep legions of marketing professionals awake at night. A new industry has come into existence just to fill the niche created by your belated desire to mate. In cities across America, copywriters work overtime to come up with new twists on one of the oldest business concepts in the world — matchmaking. And you thought your mother was the only one whose purpose in life was to get you married!

Unfortunately, many of the intended beneficiaries of all this marketing mania do not seem to be appreciative of the effort being expended in their direction. Instead, they are reacting with cynicism and scorn. They are boycotting dating services and singles organizations, believing that their cynicism is a sign of their sophistication and discrimination.

If you read Chapter 2, you know the real reason why a sophisticated and discriminating woman would avoid something as practical as a dating service. It could only be because she feels ashamed and embarrassed about wanting a relationship. That same woman, if she were looking for a housekeeper, would contact a domestic agency or place an ad in a newspaper. If she needed an employee, she would contact a placement agency or a headhunting firm.

If you've been skeptical and cynical about all the commercialization, don't be. Instead, take advantage of it. Step out into the brave new world of singles networking.

JOINING FORCES

Network: a group, system, etc. of interconnected or cooperating individuals — Webster's New World Dictionary

Networking: taking advantage of a network to get what you want

In most cities, a few hours of research will unearth enough dating services, singles dances, parties, clubs, organizations, church groups, and events to fill your calendar for the next decade. To narrow down the field, you may want to focus on networks related to your hobbies and interests.

Are you a tennis player, an art lover, a jazz enthusiast? A single parent, a chess expert? Do you like to read, ski, hike? There is probably a singles network in your city for any of these interests. By hooking up with this network, you'll not only meet men with whom you share a common interest, you'll be doing something you wanted to do anyway.

If you can't find a singles group you want to join, you can always rely on old standbys — joining a co-ed gym or taking a class.

With grocery stores jumping on the singles bandwagon, the concept of meeting men while doing something you wanted to do anyway reaches its zenith. By declaring one night a week "Singles Night," enterprising store managers are making it possible for you to pick up a man along with the rest of the items on your shopping list. Now, even something as mundane as an errand can be the occasion for an intrigue-filled night on the town. What a country!

Like with anything else, what you get out of a singles network will depend on what you put into it. Just joining isn't enough — you have to actually show up for events and make an effort to meet the men that are there.

I can't tell you how many people came into "Connecting" complaining that they had "tried networking" and hadn't met anyone. After a little probing, the truth always came out: they had dropped the ball once they had joined a network and hadn't participated in it. After "Connecting," these same people went back to the clubs or organizations they had joined and really took advantage of them. Of course, they got results.

The principles you need to apply to networking are those you learned about in Section I of this book: taking action, not letting shame and embarrassment stop you from participating, not having a chip on your shoulder, screening men in instead of out, etc. With these attitudinal tools on your side, you can't lose.

ON A PERSONAL NOTE . . .

Like a neighborhood undergoing gentrification, "the personals," once the domain of the down-and-out, have become the exclusive property of the up-and-coming. In the past, you would only have leafed through these pages if you were looking for a laugh or a weirdo. But today, by answering an ad you're more likely to find a prince than a pervert, and by placing one you may find dozens of worthy suitors. I know five couples who got married this year after meeting each other through the personals.

Personals are an updated version of college mixers — an

efficient way to connect with single people who are look-ing. Your purpose for using them should be to generate a large quantity of available men to date.

Personals provide you with a huge return on your invest-ment of time and energy by letting "your fingers do the walking." To help you get an even greater return on your investment, here are some tips on how to use the personals most effectively:

WHERE TO FIND THE BEST ONES: You'll have to do some research to find the right publications for you. Special interest group magazines, newspapers, and newsletters will help you connect with men who share your hobbies. The personals in city magazines are often geared to upscale men and women. Many cities have "singles" newspapers that are filled with page after page of personal ads, cate-gorized by interests. (These publications are also a good source of singles parties and events).

If you want to get really serious about this, you can approach it as though you were a business advertiser and find out from various publications what their demographics are. If you don't want to get that serious, just pick a news-paper or magazine you like to read.

HOW TO WRITE THEM: If you haven't already, read a bunch of ads to get a feel for them. Notice the length, content, and style of those you like, and use them as a guide when you compose yours.

The most important thing about writing your ad is to *not* list too many of those criteria you use to screen men out. Remember, the idea here is to generate the maximum *quan-tity* of men. The time to screen for quality is after you meet them. It's okay to mention some things you are looking for in a man, but don't overdo it.

HOW TO HANDLE THE RESPONSES: The key to han-dling the responses is to answer all of them. With the exception of someone who is clearly and obviously a creep, contact everyone who answers your ad. Remember, the more men you meet and date, the greater your odds of finding Mr. Right.

Lorrie did not follow this principle when she placed her personal ad a few weeks before she took "Connecting." She separated her 45 responses into a "good" pile and a "reject" pile. Seven men made it into the good pile; there were 38 rejects. She began phoning the good ones. The first got disqualified on the telephone, and the second rejected her after three promising dates. After this rejection, she didn't feel like calling anyone else.

During "Connecting," she realized that she had been overdoing it a bit with the criteria she was using to screen men out. She saw that she hadn't given the respondents enough of a chance.

She went through her two piles again. This time, only three men landed in the reject stack. She began calling the remaining respondents one by one until, midway through the pile, she met a man she really liked. She ended up marrying him later that year. They still laugh about the fact that he was originally "Reject #19."

You discovered in earlier chapters that you haven't been the greatest judge of which men are right for you even *after* you met them. How can you expect to judge a man before you meet him?

HOW TO ANSWER A MAN'S AD: If he sounds like someone you would like, don't worry about whether you fit the criteria he describes in his ad. After all, he's no better at screening women than you are at screening men. Once he meets you, he probably won't care that you're 5'3" and "voluptuous" rather than "tall and athletic."

Use your imagination. An ad Vicki read captured her interest because she found it clever and humorous. The writer jokingly said, "Nude photographs will be looked upon favorably." Vicki sent him a photograph of a Picasso nude with a funny note. Impressed with her sense of humor and curious to know what she looked like, he called her. They have been going together for six months.

Whether you answer his ad or he answers yours, one thing to avoid is an extended initial telephone conversation. After talking with someone for three hours on the phone, it can feel anti-climactic when you meet him for a date.

It's better to start out with face-to-face communication and eye contact. If you have a positive reaction to someone on the telephone, see if you can arrange a time and place to meet. Try not to stay on the phone for any longer than 10 or 15 minutes. If you're feeling spontaneous, you can say, "This sounds like fun — do you want to get in your car and meet me right now for coffee?"

BETWEEN FRIENDS

Being introduced through mutual friends or contacts is a traditional technique for meeting men that is still effective. Your own personal network of associates represents a goldmine of untapped potential. Most people have a bit of the matchmaker in them and would love to support you in your quest for a prince. Getting "fixed up" is the most comfortable way of meeting a man for many women.

Again, a few tips: You will make it easier for people to fix you up if you tell them, "Don't worry about whether you think he's my type or not — I just want to start dating." When they do fix you up, don't criticize their selection. Be gracious about the person to whom they introduced you and the experience you had, even if you spent an evening with an escapee from the Twilight Zone.

When you ask your friends to fix you up, they will often say, "Sure, I know someone great — I'll get back to you," and never call you back. You need to treat this like you would a business deal or a job or sales lead. In those cases, you would follow-up with people who didn't get back to you rather than assume they didn't mean it.

One reminder may be all it will take for them to get on the

stick. But if not, don't be afraid to bug them a little (I assume if you notice them crossing the street when they see you coming you'll know it's time to drop it). If they say they want to fix you up, take them at their word. Haven't you ever said you would do something and then it just slipped your mind?

Besides asking your friends to fix you up, you can ask them to invite you to parties or events where there are likely to be single men.

SINGLES PARTIES

Cinderella met her prince at a party, and this is still a great way to meet men. "Connecting" participants have gotten very creative about parties. A group of people who took the course in Los Angeles put together an invitation list for a party that combined their respective networks of single friends.

The invitations stipulated that there was a "cover charge" — the invitee had to bring one single and available member of the opposite sex. People were encouraged to come with friends rather than dates.

It worked! There were an even number of men and women, and because everyone knew everyone else was looking, it was very easy for people to approach each other. A lot of guests made connections. So did the hostess who has been dating a man she met at the party for the past eight months.

Don't ignore your married friends when planning singles parties. They may have single friends you can invite on their behalf.

🥿 🥿 🥿

ASSIGNMENT # 19:
CONTACT TWO SINGLES GROUPS
OR ORGANIZATIONS.

Choose two groups or events on which to do some "hands-on" research. You may want to attend a meeting, a dance, or a singles networking party. Or, you may want to shop for a dating service. You don't have to join anything, but start getting out there and seeing what's available.

ASSIGNMENT # 20:
ANSWER A PERSONAL AD.

ASSIGNMENT # 21:
WRITE AND PLACE A PERSONAL AD.
FOLLOW-UP THE RESPONSES.

The length of time this will take will depend on the number of respondents and your speed in contacting them. Don't wait too long; you want to get to them before someone else does and meet them while you're still fresh in their minds.

If no one answers your ad, it was probably written ineffectively. Try rewriting it, using ads that you like as models. Place your new ad in the same or a different publication.

ASSIGNMENT # 22:
ASK FIVE FRIENDS TO FIX YOU UP OR
TO INVITE YOU TO AN EVENT.

Don't forget to follow-up if someone doesn't get back to you after saying she or he will fix you up.

Bring On The Suitors

Notes On This Chapter:

17

"The End?"

NO, JUST THE LAST CHAPTER BEFORE THE BEGINNING.

This book has taught you how to go about finding a prince and what to do with him once you find him. From reading it, you learned the rules for the new game of relationships between men and women. Putting it into action is what will enable you to win the game.

"THE END" is when you marry your prince. This chapter is the part where I pass the ball to you. The next step is where you run with it.

Every woman who has taken "Connecting" and carried out the actions prescribed in the course has had the same result. They found relationships. Some found the prince right away; some within five or six months; others within a year. Some haven't found him yet, but they know they will because they are meeting and dating a lot of men, and they are no longer sabotaging their relationships with them.

It's going to feel like magic when you meet someone and fall in love. But it's going to take hard work to get to that point. The more you do to find a relationship, the quicker you're going to find one. The less you do, the longer it will take.

Your work is cut out for you: the assignments you've been given throughout this book will lead you to your goal. A six-week plan for completing these assignments is provided at the end of this chapter.

Feel free to add to any of the assignments. If you want to make it your goal to smile at and say hello to 100 men each week instead of 50 — great. If you want to meet five men a week instead of two or place more than one ad in the personals — terrific. The more you do, the better. If you complete all your assignments before you meet the prince, go back and do them all again.

As you work on your project during the next few months, there may come a time when you will want to quit. In Chapter 9 we discussed the fact that if you want a relationship, you have to risk rejection. After being rejected, many women feel like giving up on their projects.

Tracy met Eric about three months after "Connecting." They fell in love with each other and were practically inseparable for about six months. Then Eric decided to go back with an ex-girlfriend and it was over. This was heartbreaking for Tracy. She was not only disappointed about losing Eric, she was deeply discouraged about the whole idea of finding a relationship.

Before she met Eric, Tracy had been going out at least twice a week and doing her assignments faithfully. She had established a routine of meeting men and dating, and had built up a momentum that made it easy to keep going. After she and Eric broke up, she had to face starting all over again.

She was very tempted to give up. She said, "It never works out for me. What's the point of going out and finding another man? I don't want to have to go through this pain again. I'll never have a relationship anyway."

Luckily, Tracy had good friends who supported her through this period. They dragged her out of her house and took her to a party. They convinced her she needed to "get back on the horse." About six weeks later, Tracy met the man to whom she is now married.

If you get rejected, hang in there. What may appear to you to be a setback could be the darkness before the dawn. You may remember that I met Tony right after being rejected by another man. Tracy's experience was similar.

There may be times when you go out night after night and don't meet anyone you like for weeks. At those times, too, you may be tempted to quit. You might think, "This isn't working. I'm not getting anywhere by doing this. What's the point of continuing?"

When you feel this way, keep going. After a period of meeting no one, you'll probably get on a roll and start meeting men every time you go out.

There is no way to know how long it will take you to find your prince. I went out at least three times every week and it took me four months to meet Tony. Other women have been luckier and connected with someone right away. For others, it took a lot longer.

It is important to set a date by when you will reach your goal. Having a timeline will help you stay on track with your project and keep you from slacking off on your efforts to find a prince.

However, don't let the target date become a "deadline" that hangs over you and causes you to feel you're not making progress. Use this date to push yourself forward rather than pull yourself down.

If you reach the target date before reaching your goal, set a new date.

During the time that you are looking for a relationship, don't forget to LIVE YOUR LIFE. Enjoy your hobbies and interests. Remember, the fuller and richer your life is before you meet a man, the more you bring to your relationship with him. Enjoy the men you meet and date. Don't consider a relationship a waste of time just because it doesn't end in marriage.

≈≈ ≈≈ ≈≈

EXERCISE: STRATEGY FOR A RELATIONSHIP

The following pages will assist you in considering various aspects of your life and planning to take action on whatever you feel you need to.

STRATEGY FOR A RELATIONSHIP

CATEGORY	NEED TO DO SOMETHING	IF YES, WHAT?	BY WHEN?
1. PERSONAL APPEARANCE			
Hair •cut •color •perm			
Make-Up			
Nails			
Skin			
Regular Exercise			
Goal weight			
Teeth			
Glasses			
2. CLOTHES			
Clothes for work			

CATEGORY	NEED TO DO SOMETHING	IF YES, WHAT?	BY WHEN?
Clothes for play			
Clothes for dating			
Accessories			
3. HOME			
New place to live			
New furniture			
Repairs •to furniture •to home •need to paint			
Accessories			
Cleaning			
4. CAREER AND MONEY			
New job			
Raise			
Taxes •in order •up to date			
Investments •IRA •stocks			
Savings			
5. HOBBIES, INTERESTS			
Organizations to join			
Activities to do			

CATEGORY	NEED TO DO SOMETHING	IF YES, WHAT?	BY WHEN?
6. MEETING MEN			
Friends to support me in going out and meeting men			
Activities •personals •dating services •singles events •research to do			

Now, turn to the chart at the end of this chapter and add the action(s) you just generated to the list of assignments.

⮞⮞ ⮞⮞ ⮞⮞

The last thing I want to emphasize is the importance of support. It will make a big difference if your friends and the people around you are encouraging your project.

Those who tell you, "You shouldn't have to do anything to find a relationship; you're so special, no one's good enough for you; all the good men are taken; you're fine on your own, why look for a relationship" are not helping.

Don't listen to those people. You're probably going to come up with plenty of your own doubts — you won't need any extras. If you hang around with people who are negative about your project, it will be harder for you to keep going.

The people you should be talking to are those who, when you say, "I'm looking for a relationship" say things like, "Yes, I know it's hard, but you need to go out and do it; what are you doing this week to meet someone?; your perfect mate is out there, just keep going and you'll find him."

Many "Connecting" participants agree that the positive reinforcement they receive from the rest of the group is one of the most valuable aspects of the seminar. You will find that surrounding yourself with friends who support you will make the task before you seem less like a burden and more like an adventure.

If you've already begun carrying out your assignments, you have been working with a support partner who has been providing you with positive reinforcement all along. If you haven't found this support person yet, make sure you find one before going on to the rest of your assignments.

Believe me, you *need* this support if you're going to be successful in your project. If you don't have a partner lined up yet, re-read the instructions for assignment #1 at the end of Chapter 1, and complete that assignment before moving on to any others.

&⁓ &⁓ &⁓

ASSIGNMENT #23:
VALIDATE YOUR PROGRESS.

Schedule a meeting (or a phone call) with your support partner to review the progress you've made so far toward finding a relationship. Talk about what this project has been like for you, what you've been going through, what you've learned, what insights have been most important, and what you are most excited about. Be sure to let your partner know how her/his support has made a difference.

Don't dwell on your fears and doubts, although it's all right to mention them. The purpose of this assignment is to "empower" what you want to see more of — success in your project.

Remember in Chapter 14 when you collected evidence for your stand? The idea was to look only for those things that validated you, and no piece of evidence was too small. Apply the same principles here. Don't tell your partner that, "It was great that I overcame my fear and told that guy I found him attractive, but since he never asked me out, I guess it didn't make any difference . . ."

Don't ignore the little signs of progress — that you're smiling at men; that you told your aunt you're looking for a relationship; that you went out with someone who you didn't think was "your type;" that you bought a scarf that expresses your stand. Every step you take is getting you closer to your goal.

🥿 🥿 🥿

The last thing to do is to make a declaration about your goal. Your signature on the following statement indicates your commitment to having a relationship.

I *WILL* HAVE THE RELATIONSHIP I WANT

BY _____
date

SIGNED:_____

POSTSCRIPT

The women in "Connecting" who found princes first weren't the most beautiful ones or the ones with the best bodies or the most exciting careers. The ones who had the most success in finding relationships were those who worked the hardest and who kept going no matter what.

The road you're taking has peaks and valleys, dips and turns — but it *is* the right road. Stay on it. The only way you can fail in your project is by giving up.

GOOD LUCK!

SIX-WEEK ACTION PLAN FOR FINDING A PRINCE

WEEK ONE

Find a partner/support person.

(p. 17) _____

Tell five people you're looking for a relationship. (p. 25) _____

Do what is necessary to be ready for a relationship. (p. 51) _____

Take one action this week to find a relationship. (p. 52) _____

Smile at and say hello to 50 men.

(p. 52) _____

OTHER: _____

WEEK TWO

Do something about your looks.

(p. 39) _____

Take one action this week to find a relationship. (p. 52)* _____

Smile at and say hello to 50 men.

(p. 52)* _____

Meet two new men this week.

(p. 73) _____

*repeat assignment

Ask five friends to fix you up or to invite you
to an event.   (p. 201)   _____

Validate your progress.

(p. 209)   _____

OTHER:

WEEK THREE

Do something now to become, do, feel, or
have what you've been waiting for.

(p. 38)   _____

Do something "out of character".

(p. 38)   _____

Take one action this week to find a relationship.   (p. 52)*   _____

Smile at and say hello to 50 men.

(p. 52)*   _____

Meet two new men this week.

(p. 73)*   _____

Compliment one man each day.

(p. 165)   _____

Purge your closet.

(p. 181)   _____

OTHER: _____

*repeat assignment

WEEK FOUR

Take one action this week to find a rela-
tionship.   (p. 52)*   _____

Smile at and say hello to 50 men.
                                             (p. 52)*   _____

Meet two new men this week.
                                             (p. 73)*   _____

Tell a man you find him attractive.
                                             (p. 120)   _____

Plan a party.   (p. 151)   _____

Interview two happily married couples
about their marriage.
                                             (p. 190)   _____

Validate your progress*
                                             (p. 209)   _____

OTHER: _____

WEEK FIVE

Take one action this week to find a rela-
tionship.   (p. 52)*   _____

Smile and say hello to 50 men.
                                             (p. 52)*   _____

Meet two new men this week.
                                             (p. 73)*   _____

*repeat assignment

Collect one piece of evidence each day for
your stand.   (p. 181)   _____

Do one thing to have your appearance reflect
your stand.   (p. 182)   _____

Create a relationship "portrait".

(p. 189)   _____

Answer a personal ad.

(p. 200)   _____

OTHER: _____

WEEK SIX

Take one action this week to find a relationship.   (p. 52)*   _____

Smile at and say hello to 50 men.

(p. 52)*   _____

Meet two new men this week.*

(p. 73)   _____

Get intimate with a man.

(p. 151)   _____

Contact two singles groups or organizations
(p. 200)   _____

Write and place a personal ad.

(p. 200)   _____

Validate your progress.*

(p. 209)   _____

OTHER: _____

*repeat assignment

SEMINARS OFFERED BY NITA TUCKER

CONNECTING: How to Find a Lifetime Relationship

This two-day course is designed for people who want to find nurturing, loving, and romantic relationships. The Connecting Seminar takes this book one step further through personalized coaching, a structured format, and the support provided by a group. In the course, individuals have an opportunity to pursue issues of specific relevance to them and to become more effective in finding relationships.

CONNECTING II: The Art and Science of Extraordinary Relationships

To maintain a successful, lasting relationship requires skill and dedication. Connecting II is a two-day course for couples who want their relationships to be extraordinary and who are willing to do what it takes to achieve that result.

The course provides tools, exercises and techniques that will help people deal effectively with issues that typically arise in long-term relationships — communication, finances, children, sex, etc. It teaches couples how to make their relationships passionate, fun, and romantic.

TO ORDER MORE COPIES OF *BEYOND CINDERELLA:*
The Modern Woman's Guide to Finding a Prince,
call: 1-800-445-MATE.
In Washington state, call (206) 328-7840.